PRAISE for Co~~i~~

Professi~~onal Services~~

"As someone in the business of advising on customer loyalty, it's nice to see a book on sales that actually takes an honest and authentic approach to sales that improves trust and relationships. I also enjoyed Richard's easy to read conversational style, some great analogies and live examples, plus the practical exercises that make it easy for us to implement the principles in our own businesses."

Caroline Cooper, Naturally Loyal

"A practical guide to consultative selling packed with useful structures, tips and anecdotes which are simple to understand and apply immediately into your sales activity. Read it thoroughly or use it as a reference guide which you dip in and out of, either way you'll get great guidance on how you to improve results from your sales activity as a consultant."

Derek Bishop, Culture Consultancy

"If you are struggling to grow a new consultancy or want to take your professional services firm to the next level, I thoroughly recommend 'Consultative Selling for Professional Services'; the techniques it contains will transform your business."

Dylan Jones, DataQualityPro.com

"The strategies within this book have enabled me to better understand the ideal type of client for d2 Solutions, what would make them decide to buy from me rather than anyone else, and why they are willing to pay higher fees necessary for sustained business growth. As a result I now feel much more in control of the sales of our business, and we have been able to attract and win a number of clients with the kinds of projects that previously had been elusive."

Dave Nyss, d2 Solutions

"I am quite confident in sales but that does not mean I win as much business as I should. This book has helped me to understand the importance of following a structured sales process, and I can see a few important areas where I am going wrong. I plan to make it required reading for all my consultants."

Sharif George, Cloudberry

"This book explains how consultative selling plays to a consultant's strengths and helps you 'close' the sale by helping your prospect—not selling to them. Not only do I find this approach highly successful—I really enjoy it, too! So if you shudder at the thought of selling, then this book is a must."

Chantal Cooke, Panpathic Communications

"As a 30-year-veteran sales professional, I thought I knew it all when it came to sales and selling. However, since launching myself as a consultant I have found selling my own expertise to be completely new territory. Richard has written a book that has really captured the value of consultative selling, and most importantly, shown me how to use it effectively to build my personal development consultancy business."

Dene Stuart, I Want to Be

"This book encapsulates so clearly and succinctly the vital elements of consultative selling. I particularly like Chapter Four, 'The WHY factor', which gets to the essence of how to move from selling to helping clients buy from you. It is now required reading at SciVisum."

Deri Jones, SciVisum Ltd

"In the financial services industry we are going through a big transition where we now earn our income from selling our advice rather than selling products. This book provides financial planners with a structured way to sell their services with integrity and without needing to be pushy."

Dr. Lien Luu, Senior Lecturer in Financial Services & Certified & Chartered Financial Planner, University of Northampton

"Closing the sale is sometimes a challenge for our clients, especially those offering professional services like dentistry. This book shows how to close the sale in a professional and respectful manner, and I will be recommending it to my clients."

Nat Schooler, Getwise Marketing

"Richard has helped to completely demystify sales and the process of selling. I can now confidently handle a sales conversation that involves the purchase of a premium product."

John Cassidy, The Headshot Guy®

"This is a great book for anyone who is in the business of selling their own expertise and know-how. I like how Richard gives the bigger picture and helps the reader understand the why and not just the how."

Nigel Wyatt, Magenta Financial Training

"I found the book informative, well balanced, enjoyable to read, and I am confident it will help me improve my consultative selling. I will definitely be referring to this book on a regular basis."

Rob Darwin, Digital Mail Ltd

"The book contains a great process/approach and encourages technical experts that selling is not to be feared and indeed can be enjoyable."

Bhupendra Patel, ZenStrat Consulting

"Another great book by Richard White. I like how it gives a bird's eye view of sales for professionals and then goes down into the detail. Even though I consider myself moderately competent at sales, I still gained several new insights with practical applications."

Andrew Horder, Business coach and consultant

"This book is invaluable and has given me the confidence that I am approaching 'sales' visits in the right manner, not with the objective of selling to a prospect but of positioning myself to become their trusted adviser. I also refer to it before each 'sales' visit to make sure the techniques are fresh in my mind."

Chris Burton-Brown, Mylor Financial Management Ltd

"An excellent book that delivers a simple seven step approach to consultative selling. Before reading this book I found even thinking about selling a stressful experience. I can now see how, if it is done properly, it compliments my approach of helping my clients solve their problems. I particularly like the exercises that help you implement this approach yourself and the links to more useful resources on the author's website. Instead of feeling apprehensive about sales, I'm now looking forward to the opportunity to try out these techniques."

Nicola Askham, Data Governance Coach

Consultative Selling for Professional Services

The Essential Sales Manual for Consultants and Other Trusted Advisers

Richard White

Acknowledgements

I thank Peter Aggleton and Mark Gee for taking a big risk with me back in 1997 and believing that I had promise as a business developer, even when I gave them reason to believe otherwise. I learnt a lot about sales and sales management from Peter, who is a true professional with integrity to match.

As you read through this book you will quickly notice that I talk a lot about my mentors and the impact they have had on my sales over the years. I use the term mentoring loosely in relation to people who have shaped the way I think rather than teach me what to do. I find that in life, and especially in sales, when I understand the right way to think then the 'how to' becomes fairly easy. In this regard I have to give a special thank you to Brian Harrison, who was my first sales mentor and who took me under his wing and gave valuable feedback in my early sales meetings.

It seems a bit of a cliché to thank my clients, but the truth is that everything I have learnt that really matters in consultative selling comes from modelling others. I am especially grateful for Andrew Douglas of Newhall Publications for commissioning a full NLP modelling exercise on his sales team back in 2003. Although it was for door-to-door selling rather than consultative selling, the research led to my work around Client Archetypes and WOW! Goals and my understanding about helping people overcome sales reluctance.

For my work on storytelling, I thank Espen Holm for his mentoring. Espen, in a former life, was an accomplished sales person for IBM and is now a full time storyteller in Norway and has written many excellent books. Thomas Power, co-founder of Ecademy.com gave me valuable mentoring on effective networking.

I also thank Sue Knight and Ian Ross for my first introduction to NLP back in 1993 and for 'selling' me on the idea of modelling excellence in others. This book is based on my model of consultative selling, and it is the book that I wish I had back in 1997 when I first started out as a principal consultant.

A big thank you to my many other teachers in NLP and NLP Coaching over the last twenty years, who have all had their impact on this subject area in some way—especially in the area of communication and influence, and modeling excellence. These include Richard Bandler, John Grinder, Robert Dilts, Tad James, Christina Hall, Wyatt Woodsmall, Paul McKenna, Michael Breen, Ian McDermott, and Lisa Turner.

Tim Robinson gets a special mention and thank you for introducing me more fully into the works of Miller Heiman and complex sales of which I continue to be an advocate.

A big thanks for Daniel Priestly and his excellent 'Become a Key Person of Influence' program which I attended back in 2011 and which gave me the confidence and roadmap to specialise in working with consultants and trusted advisors.

This is the book I should have written back in 2011; it has taken a long time to properly articulate my message. The truth is that I made my first attempt at writing this book almost ten years ago, and I have a disk full of half-written books that have been abandoned over the years.

I am grateful to Lucy Whittington for helping me to discover 'my thing,' which is helping people understand who their ideal clients are and why they buy from them. That led to my 5-Star-Client methodology, and as it turned out, was the thing needed to ensure this book has something new to say on the subject of Consultative Selling.

I would like to thank Topher Morrison for his Legacy professional speakers program that I attended in 2011 and the subsequent mentoring on professional speaking.

Finally, I would like to thank my wife, Caroline, for her patience and support. I am sure she is in disbelief that this book is finally finished!

Contents

Introduction

It was 14th July, 1997. I remember the day vividly as it was the day I became an accidental salesman. I had been a technical consultant working for the software giant, Oracle, and I wanted to be a principal consultant. I wanted the extra money. I thought my technical skills were good enough, and my clients liked me and gave me extra work. I was what I now know to be a *trusted adviser*. However, I did not get a promotion, and when a friend called me saying that he was working in a medium-sized IT consultancy and wanted to develop an Oracle practice, I grasped the opportunity to become a principal consultant.

Unfortunately, I had not anticipated how much sales would be involved. Most of their existing Oracle business was coming directly from Oracle on a sub-contracted basis, and they wanted me to help them gain more direct clients. On 14th July, 1997 I discovered that 'business development' is what consultants call 'sales' to make themselves feel better about it. I had fallen in the deep end, and on top of having to do sales, I was also expected to cover my rather large salary by doing my own consulting work—which I had to find!

I really hated the idea of sales, and I managed to get my company to pay for some sales training and sales coaching. In fact, they were very generous with the training; but unfortunately, it just made things worse. It all just seemed so manipulative, and the trainers were proper sales people rather than technical consultants. I enjoyed the trust of clients, and I could see that using these tactics with my clients would go down like a lead balloon and blow the trust they placed in me. They would stop seeing me as a trusted adviser and start treating me like any other sales person. When I was at Oracle, I used to be onsite working with clients who would tell me what they thought about the sales people. I did not want to be one of those people. Besides, I doubted they would ever give me consulting work for myself unless they liked and trusted me.

I actually nearly gave up on more than one occasion, but fortunately, my ambition kept me going—along with the thought of having to return to being a senior consultant or follow the life of an independent contractor. My fortunes began to turn when I managed to persuade a colleague who was very successful at sales to mentor me on an unofficial basis. What I liked about his style was that it was very professional, and it did not even seem like he was selling when he spoke to clients. He helped me to change the way I thought about certain aspects of sales. At the same time I was reading a lot of books around subjects like people skills, communication, and influence, as well as more straightforward sales books. My mentor recommended some of those to me.

Eventually, I found other mentors, and over a three-year period I was able to win and build up some significant 'blue chip' clients, including Unilever, British Airways, and First Choice. The income stream from my clients became an important part of the consulting business, continuing long after I had left the company. More importantly, I went from hating selling to loving it. I enjoyed the learning and personal development and the challenge of developing my own style of selling. I knew that I wanted to run my own consulting business one day, although at that point I had assumed it would be an IT consulting business.

As it happened, friends running their own businesses saw the improvements and started asking for my advice and help. I started mentoring them in a similar way that I had been mentored, and they started to make big improvements too. They said that when I explained things to them it all made sense. Then I started to be recommended to their friends, until one day someone asked me how much I charged! I had never seen it as a business prior to this. To me it was just giving back what had been kindly given to me by my various mentors. So I made up a number, and the rest is history!

Over the last eleven years as a sales consultant, I have worked with a whole variety of different businesses, from one-man-bands struggling to find their first client to blue chip organisations wanting their sales people to adopt a consultative approach. I have been fortunate to have worked with some very successful sales people, who I have found do not tend to fit the normal 'pushy' sales person stereotype. I have continued to learn and develop through research into best practice, and I love being able to share that research in a simple and straightforward manner.

What I learned from all my research is that consultants can be great at business development if they focus on applying their consulting skills to sales rather than thinking they need to be a pushy sales person. Taking a systematic and strategic approach to sales and developing the right mindset will mean that you can become very successful at business development over time without having to lose your integrity and resort to pushy and manipulative tactics. Indeed, if you want to make selling easy, this is the right book for you.

This is not just another book on consultative selling. This is a book specifically for trusted advisers who want to quickly master sales and feel comfortable with selling so that they can spend more time being a trusted adviser. Consultative selling is a subject that is taught widely, although not necessarily taught well; many clients come to me having had a lot of training in consultative selling and yet they do not seem to understand the basics.

When you master the basics of consultative selling and you develop the right mindset, then it is incredibly easy. In this book I start with the absolute fundamentals and focus on helping you understand why they are important. My aim is to provide the essence of the learning gained from mentors over the years combined with many years' experience of making consultative selling work for both myself, team members, and clients.

This book is about understanding the basics of consultative selling and the consultative selling mindset. It does not matter how many years' experience you have, if your sales results are not where you want them to be or you do not feel comfortable and in control of your sales the answers will be in those fundamentals rather than with 'clever' and manipulative tactics. Moreover, I truly believe that anyone with the motivation to learn and develop can follow the teachings in this book and be successful at consultative selling.

If you are reading this and you have already had lots of training in consultative selling, I believe you will still get some great new ideas. Perhaps it will be on how to find new clients or get existing clients to spend more money with you. Perhaps it will be how to feel much better about sales and boost your activity. And most likely you will get to understand why your clients really buy from you and how to use that knowledge in winning even more sales.

Chapters One and Two give a high-level introduction to the consultative sales approach and the mechanics of selling. Then, in Chapters Three and Four, I cover a critical element of sales that is so often neglected: understanding who your clients are and why they buy from you. Chapters Five and Six are related to finding and winning more business; Chapters Seven to Nine cover the process of consultative selling in more detail. Finally, Chapter Ten is about developing your skill through to mastery.

I recommend you read this book with an open mind and that where you see exercises you have a go at doing them. This is probably a book that you will read more than once. If you are not getting the results you want, the answer you need will be in one of the chapters and so you may need to come back and look at the relevant one(s) in more detail. Please also check out the resources section where, in addition to recommended further reading, you will get a link to www.theaccidentalsalesman.com where you can get free online video mini-courses which will build upon what you learn in this book.

This is the book I wish I had back in 1997. Although I was not that enthusiastic about sales back then, I have now learnt to love it and it has impacted positively all areas of my life. I wish the same for you.

Best wishes,
Richard White

Chapter One

A Professional Way to Sell Services

Introduction

It was Peter's sixth birthday, and as a special treat his father had taken him to the local park to feed the pigeons. Peter had heard from his school friends that it was possible to have pigeons eat from your hand and that is what Peter intended to do today. His father handed him a few slices of bread, and clutching them tightly, Peter began to run towards a group of hungry looking pigeons, shouting, "'Dinnertime! Dinnertime! Come and get some lovely bread!"

As Peter approached, all the pigeons flew away. The more he tried, the more pigeons left the park. Peter finally bowed his head, bit his lip and began to sob.

His father came over and put his arm around the little boy and said, "Here, Peter, let me show you how it's done."

As Peter watched, his father broke off a few pieces of bread and slowly began sprinkling them on the ground. Peter saw that his father just ignored the pigeons. After a little while, a couple of curious birds came forward and began to peck cautiously at the bread, all the time checking to make sure it was safe. Gradually, the birds sensed it was safe and came a little closer, eating the crumbs as they advanced; all the time they were checking for danger, poised to fly at any moment. The father gently lowered his hand and very carefully opened his palm to display the crumbs within. Before long one pigeon eased forward and began to peck at the crumbs in his hand. Then another pigeon came forward, followed by another and another. Soon the whole area around the father and son was covered in pigeons, all flying in from the local neighbourhood.

In this chapter I will reveal the secret of finding clients who want to buy from you rather than you having to chase after them. You will see how easy business development can be if you go with human nature rather than work against it. You will learn why there is no need to be pushy and manipulative, and indeed, why selling with integrity and using a consultative approach is much more effective.

Push selling vs pull selling

Some people wonder what the difference is between business development and sales. When I landed my first business development role, I quickly discovered that there is no difference. The common joke around business development is that it's the label you use for people who dislike the idea of selling! I hope that by the time you finish reading this book you will feel more comfortable about the idea of sales. It took me many years to develop an approach that I felt comfortable with, and business developers I shared the approach with also became more comfortable. I refer to it as 'soft selling', but essentially, it's a style of what's known as 'consultative selling'.

From my research into the different selling styles and strategies around, there are effectively two different approaches, which are really down to the attitude of the person doing the selling; they are 'push' selling and 'pull' selling.

'Push' selling is the approach that I see everywhere and that causes us to think a sales person is being pushy. In push selling, the focus is the product or service that we are seeking to sell and we push it onto the market. I know this, because it is how I once sold. I copied everyone else around me, and even some of my best mentors did this. The attitude is that we sell the product and the skill is getting someone to buy.

You can do push selling without being pushy. Push selling is where our approach to selling is to just talk about our services and how great they are. This style of selling might work if you are selling a commodity to an educated buyer, but I am assuming that you and your colleagues know more about your area of expertise than your clients and prospects. Talking about our services and how great they are is important, but it has to be done at the right point in the sales process.

Sell like a doctor

The best way to sell professional services is using an approach called 'consultative selling'. The good news is that consultants find it much easier to do than do normal sales people. People who are really good at consultative selling are doctors selling a patient a solution to their medical problem.

Imagine going to a doctor with a medical problem. You would expect the doctor to ask some questions and maybe do some tests in order to diagnose your condition. Then the doctor would prescribe a course of treatment that they believed would solve your problem.

The process is similar to the consultative sales process, where you look for prospects with problems you are able to solve. You then find out more so that you can correctly understand the problem before recommending a solution.

Push selling is like a doctor deciding what drugs they want to prescribe even before they get to meet patients. The patient is likely to get suspicious when the doctor makes their diagnosis without asking any questions or doing any tests.

Even when people come to you asking about your services, you should still take a step back and take them through a similar process to the one the doctor follows, just to ensure that anything you recommend is going to work for them. Otherwise, it would be like a doctor writing a prescription for powerful drugs just because a patient thinks they need them. In sales this is referred to as 'order taking'.

Be a trusted adviser

The 'Holy Grail' in sales is for your clients to see you as their trusted adviser, and consultative selling, when done well, will deliver this for you. Your clients will want to come to you to discuss their problems, which will give you an advantage over your competitors. However, you are unlikely to be the first person they call if they think you are more interested in the sale than in helping them solve their problems. Consultative selling engenders trust when you take prospects through the process before making your recommendation. The good news is that it is also easier to do, especially for those people who hate the idea of being pushy or manipulative.

A trusted adviser has the benefit that prospects and clients are happy to talk openly to them about their problems. They will reveal things they would never reveal to a normal sales person. They will also be happy to take your calls and be honest about what is going on. Whilst you may not always win every project, you are more likely to win work where there is a good fit, and you will not have to do all the chasing that regular pushy sales people end up doing when their prospect goes quiet.

We need to change the way we think about sales. Instead of looking for people who want our services, we need to look for people who have problems in achieving the results they want.

Problems we can fix. We attract them by showing that we may be able to solve their problems. Once they step forward and start to ask questions, we will have a process for helping them to gain confidence in our ability to solve their problems, and they will happily engage our services.

What's the problem?

A simple example of the contrast between push selling and pull selling happened one day a few years ago, when I went shopping for a new flat screen TV. Close to where I live, there are two large electrical retailers within a five-minute walk of each other. I walked into the first shop and told the assistant that I was looking for a flat screen TV. He immediately started raving about the latest TV on the market. I could see the price quite clearly on display and said it was a little bit out of my price range. Instead of finding out what I was looking for, he just started raving about another TV. This is push selling.

Contrast this with my experience at the other shop. The assistant was very similar, but in this case he asked me if I wanted a particular screen size, and whether I had a particular price range. He also asked me if I had a colour preference. (Most of the TVs looked similar—kind of black—but there were some that were in a silver frame.) When I answered his questions, he gave me the options. I made my decision, paid the money, and left. This was a much better example of consultative selling. The assistant found out what I wanted and sold it to me. Yet it would have been even better if he had asked me *why* I wanted the new TV. If he had taken the trouble to discover my buying motivation, it is possible that that he could have recommended some additional products as well.

Mind the gap

As a good consultant, you are probably used to asking questions and gathering information before giving your best advice.

23

'Consultative selling' requires you to act like a consultant during the sales process. Being a good consultant, you want first to discover your client's problems and **then** give your best advice. In sales you need to do exactly the same. First, you need to attract people who have problems you can solve. Then you find out more about the problems. Only then can you present a credible solution. Where people often go wrong in consultative selling is that they have already decided what the solution is, and then they work hard to convince the prospect to buy the solution. This is just push selling.

In consultancy we have a tool called 'gap analysis', which is used to determine the gap between where the client wants to be and where they currently are. I will go into this in much detail in Chapter Eight, but for now I will just say that we are seeking to find the gap between the results the client wants and their current situation. The gap shows us how much value we are able to add with our services. If there is no gap between what they want and their current situation, then there is no real motivation to change, and a sale is highly unlikely.

Going back to the flat screen TV example, what the first sales person did not know is that the TV was to go into a new cabinet and there was a specific size restriction. There was definitely a budget restriction, and also, as it happened, a colour preference. The second sales person discovered this because he asked the appropriate questions and let my wife and I do the talking.

When we take the focus away from ourselves and what we will get from the sale and instead focus on the client and learning how we can help them solve their problems, it all becomes so much easier. We do not sell anything until we know why they have expressed an interest in speaking to us and why they may be interested in buying our services. We have a number of stages to go through before we even know exactly what we are selling, and at any one of those stages we, or the prospective client, may decide not to proceed any further.

When we follow this selling style properly we do not feel like we are selling and the client does not feel like they are being sold to. The prospective client knows we have their best interests at heart and as a result they begin to place their trust in us; we are then on our way to developing the status of trusted adviser rather than being seen as a pushy sales person who cannot be trusted.

Buying motives

If we want to be successful in selling business-to-business professional services, we need to come from the mindset that our clients are not interested in buying our services and would rather save the expense. They engage our services because they believe these services will deliver more benefit to the business than they cost. However, when people contact us about our services they are probably not thinking directly about how we can help them increase profits. They are more likely to be thinking about something more specific they want help with. It's only when we are trying to gain a commitment from them to spend money that the need for a return on investment will become essential. However, we do need to be aware of it at all times to ensure we do not waste too much time pursuing sales opportunities where we are unable to add enough value to justify the client in going ahead.

So while increasing profits or minimising losses will be motivators, there will be more specific motivation. Using outsourced HR consultancy as an example, there may be many different motivations for potential clients to want to engage in a sales conversation, such as:

- They already buy HR support services, but their existing supplier is not responsive enough.

- The organisation may be growing and experiencing people problems that they are unable to deal with.

- They may be bidding for government contracts and have compliance issues that need to be resolved.

- They may be experiencing a specific HR issue that they need some professional input to resolve.

- They may be downsizing and need help in handling the HR-related consequences.

- They may want to make sure they are doing everything properly so that they keep staff happy and do not expose themselves to any risks of expensive employment tribunals.

When we understand the specific buying motive that has caused a client or potential client to want to talk to us, it becomes easier to know how to handle the sale. We do not have to push anything. All we have to do is to use our consulting skills to discover more about the problem and then present a viable solution, whilst recognising that we need to be able to show a return on investment and demonstrate why working with us is their best option. With consultative selling, there is no need to push provided you know there is a strong motivation to buy. And if there is no buying motivation then you can be sure there will not be a sale, and so pushing will be futile anyway!

There is a specific process for taking a sales opportunity from an initial expression of interest all the way through to closing the sale. We will be covering the process in Chapter Two, and for the remainder of the book, buying motivation will be a major theme. It is a key component of what I call the business development 'groundwork'.

Doing the groundwork

If we want to build a solid house, it is important that we first lay solid foundations. The same is true for business development. The foundations for successful business development for professional services are to gain clarity as to the following key areas:

- Who are your ideal clients?
- Why do they buy the services you provide?
- How do your services add value?
- Why would they buy from you rather than a competitor?
- How can you prove you can deliver?

Who are your ideal clients?

There will be certain clients where there is a very good mutual fit. These are what I call your 5-Star Clients. These clients will be easier to win and they are more likely to provide you with a regular stream of work and referrals. Being clear as to who are your 5-Star Clients will make selling easier and more time efficient for you. We will be identifying your 5-Star Clients in Chapter Three.

Why do they buy the services you provide?

We have seen above that buying motivation is an important aspect in consultative selling, and we will be covering it in greater detail in Chapter Four.

How do your services add value?

To be successful at consultative selling we need to have a very clear sense of how we add value to our clients. This will help us to determine whether a particular sales opportunity is worth pursuing and it will also help us to better justify charging higher rates than our clients might be expecting. We will be dealing with value propositions in Chapter Four.

Why would they buy from you rather than a competitor?

As a consultant you may find that you are competing with some large brands who field very well trained sales people. However, you can still win easily when you are clear as to what your competitive edge is with your ideal clients, and we will also be dealing with this in Chapter Four.

How can you prove you can deliver?

It is possible to generate a lot of interest in your services, but without credibility it is unlikely you will close the sale. In Chapter Four we will be covering how you can make the most of, and build on, your existing credibility.

Summary

There is no need to be pushy or manipulative to be successful at selling professional services. Indeed, the total opposite is required if we want to be regarded as a trusted adviser by our clients. Rather than trying to push our services onto clients and prospects, we need to be getting into a position where our clients and prospects are coming to us to buy our services. We do this by working with their buying motivation and taking them through the consultative sales process, which involves taking time to understand their problem and then proposing a solution. To make the consultative sales process work, we need to have clarity about our ideal clients, why they buy from us, and how they benefit from working with us.

> For free resources on **Consultative Selling for Professional Services**, including free mini-course, webinars, and e-books, visit **www.theaccidentalsalesman.com**

Chapter Two

The Mechanics of Consultative Selling

Introduction

Now that you are involved with business development, you have a need to generate a consistent stream of client work for yourself and your colleagues. It is, therefore, critical that you take a systematic approach to business development rather than leaving it to chance. This is especially important if you need time for delivering client work, so that you avoid the 'feast and famine' cycle, where you only get involved in business development activity out of desperation. In this chapter I will show you how to build a sales machine that will deliver you quality business, month in and month out. You will learn the various components of your sales machine and what it takes to make it all work.

The sales sausage machine

Have you ever seen one of those old-fashioned cast iron sausage machines? They have a long barrel, a hopper on the top, and a big handle on the side. You put the sausage meat in the hopper, turn the handle, and out the end of the barrel comes a string of sausages. If you keep the hopper well supplied with sausage meat and keep turning the handle, the sausages will keep on coming.

As the sausage meat travels through the machine, it undergoes a process in order to be transformed into a sausage. The sausage meat is equivalent to a sales opportunity and your sales sausage machine is there to convert sales opportunities into confirmed project work. Just like the sausage meat, a sales opportunity is taken through a series of stages whereby it is transformed and becomes ready to move on to the next stage.

You can have the best sales sausage machine in the world, but unless you replenish the sausage meat that has been processed, you will eventually run out and your supply of new sausages will cease. Many consulting firms suffer from the 'feast and famine' syndrome. They are short of work, and in a state of mad panic and desperation they look for sales opportunities. It takes time for sales opportunities to go through the transformation process, and everyone is praying that they will turn into firm consulting work. Eventually, some of them do and now all the focus switches to delivering the consulting work. The business development activity slows down and ceases, and the firm is doomed to repeat the same process all over again once the current consulting projects have been completed.

It is much better for the heart and the bank balance to get in the habit of continually filling the sausage machine, especially when you are very busy. Rather than stop seeking leads, you can be much more effective by being better targeted and very fussy about the sales opportunities you pursue. When a business is suffering a sales famine they tend to pursue opportunities that they would not even consider if they had plenty of work. It gets very time effective if you target your new business activities toward your ideal clients and focus on the type of sales opportunities that do not take a lot of time initially, but that will grow into a source of regular work in the future.

The components of your sales sausage machine

Continuing with the analogy of the sales sausage machine, there are various components that make the sausage making process work. These are:

- The hopper—the mechanism through which the sausage meat is fed into the machine (sales lead generation).

- The barrel—the mechanism for transforming the sausage meat into sausages (sales process).

- The handle—the mechanism for moving the sausage meat through the barrel (sales activity).

The great thing is that when business development is done correctly it becomes easier to fill the sales sausage machine because a good proportion of the sales leads should come from your existing clients in the form of project extensions, additional projects, and referrals.

Your ideal clients should be a major source of new business, and so it is important to understand how each stage works and the role buying motivation plays at each stage.

The consultative sales process

A sale should naturally go through each of the following stages:

1. Generate Interest
2. Qualify Interest
3. Discover Wants and Needs
4. Propose Solution
5. Negotiate Solution
6. Ask for the Business
7. Deliver the Promise

It is critically important that you take the sale through each of the stages one-by-one in the right order to maximise the chances of winning the sale and creating follow-on sales opportunities. The stages in the sales process all build on each other, and a sales opportunity only passes to the next stage once it has satisfied specific 'exit' criteria. Rather than push an opportunity through the sales process, the prospect's buying motivation gives the sales opportunity its own momentum, and you just need to be able to help guide the sales opportunity through the process.

Generate Interest

The first stage of the sales process is to generate some kind of interest in having a sales conversation, even if it is just a spark of interest. You are looking for businesses with problems that you can fix by providing your services. Your lead generation activity should result in people putting up their hand and letting you know that they have such a problem and would like to talk to you about how you can potentially help them. They are not asking to buy your services at this stage, but they are interested in solving their problem. With any luck, they have already allocated a budget to solving the problem, but there again, they may not have done so yet. You will discover why not having a budget is not necessarily a problem in Chapter Four.

Interest could manifest itself in a variety of ways. For example:

- An existing client mentions a problem during a conversation.

- An introducer makes an introduction following a discussion.

- A potential client makes a website enquiry asking about prices.

- You get an email enquiry asking for more information.

- You have a conversation where you are asked about a particular service.

These are all expressions of interest, and they should alert you to the fact that the person may be in buying mode. However, there is a big difference between being in buying mode and being ready to buy. We cannot sell at this stage because we do not know what we are selling. We just want our clients and potential clients to be interested in talking to us about what we can do to help them solve their problems.

The criteria for moving from Generate Interest to Qualify Interest will be where contact has been made and they have agreed to speak with you. You should be aiming to have a brief conversation on the telephone as soon as possible. A lot of opportunities are lost by relying on email correspondence, and you should seek to get a commitment to a telephone call.

Qualify Interest

Once you have an expression of interest, the next stage is to make sure that there is actually a sales opportunity and there is a good fit with what your organisation is able to offer. This is a stage that business developers rarely do well. They are so excited at getting some interest in their services that they do not take the time to check whether there is a proper sales opportunity. As we proceed during the various stages of the sales process we need to continually question whether there is a real sales opportunity for us or whether we are wasting our time. The 'Qualify Interest' stage is an initial check before investing time in a sales meeting.

When you are busy with billable project work, it is easy to attach a cost to attending sales meetings—but you also need to consider what else you could be using the time for. When you include travelling, you may spend half a day or more on the meeting, and so it is vitally important that you qualify interest.

I can remember vividly the day I learnt my lesson as to the value of this stage in the sales process. It was back in my IT consulting days. Like many other people, I had heard about the need to qualify but given I did not have many sales opportunities, I would not bother. Then one day I drove five hours for a 'hot sales appointment' my telemarketing company had generated for me, only to discover that the person was on holiday! I felt sickened, and on my five-hour journey back I vowed never to do that again.

Imagine what would have happened if the sales meeting had gone ahead. He obviously did not have much interest, and it probably would have ended with him asking me to send him a proposal. I would have spent half a day writing a proposal, only to find that he had disappeared off the planet. Just imagine all the time I would have wasted.

Time is the key reason why you need to qualify interest. You want to make sure you are not going to be wasting either your time or the prospect's time by getting into a sales conversation. A great test is to imagine you are so busy that you are unable to take on much more business. Would you still progress with this sales conversation or would it be a waste of time?

Other information you may also want to glean includes whether they have a budget, the timescales they are looking at, and—critically—who else would be involved in making the ultimate decision. The wording you use to find out this information should be scripted, tested, and evolved to become what works best for what you are selling. For example, getting a prospect to specify their budget early in the sales process can be a struggle. However, all you need to know is that they have one or that getting a budget is not going to be a problem. One of the many ways of achieving this is to give a range that matches the typical budget requirement:

"Our client projects normally come out somewhere between £5,000 and £50,000—will that be an issue for you?"

I was taught to always ask who was the decision maker and almost always got the answer, "That's me!" only to find that there was someone else who had to approve the expenditure. The level of authority will change depending on the size of sale, and as we will see later, our first sale is going to be relatively small. Nevertheless, we should get the information by asking,

"Who else will need to be involved in the decision to go ahead with a project like this?"

It is critical to find out this information at this stage or else you risk getting in a situation later down the line where you are getting information second hand and relying on someone else to get the decision maker to decide to go ahead. We should never rely on someone else to put our solutions across in the best light.

In reality, this stage is an initial qualification, and you will need to continually sense-check as you proceed through later stages of the sales process to ensure you are not wasting your time. It's about 'testing the water' and going into the discovery phase of the sales process with your eyes open and the confidence that your time will be well spent. I find that busy people prefer to have a ten-minute telephone conversation prior to arranging a sales meeting because they do not want to waste their time either.

Discovering the buying motivation at this stage not only ensures that there is a potential sale, but also opens out the conversation. In Chapter Four we will explore buying motivation in depth and consider how to find it. For now I will just say that we check for buying motivation by asking a simple question to determine why they are interested in having a sales conversation. The question will be simple, but the answer will speak volumes and provide clues about how best to handle the sale or, indeed, whether it is worth continuing to the next phase.

You may have lower qualification criteria with existing clients, but to proceed to the 'Discover Wants and Needs' stage you should be confident that there is a suitable potential sales opportunity there. You do not have to be precise, but you do need to be sure that you are not wasting your time. As you progress through this book and complete the exercises you will begin to gain clarity as to what is a good sales opportunity for you, and so this section should make a lot more sense the second time around.

Discover Wants and Needs

The discovery phase of the sales process is often viewed as a sales meeting, and with smaller projects it can be a meeting with just one person. It could alternatively be a meeting with several people, or it may not be a physical meeting at all; it could instead be a conference call or even a series of meetings and calls. We are still not selling at this stage; instead we are gathering the information we need and probing to find out more. I will look at this stage in depth in Chapter Eight. For now I will say that, for new business, we are looking to establish trust and credibility, and to discover all we need to make a very compelling proposal. Addressing their buying motivation as well as other important buying criteria is what will make the proposal compelling, and so it is important that we not only discover what they need, but also what they want. Indeed, it is quite likely that they will be unclear of what they actually need to solve their problem, but they may have an idea of the result they are seeking.

Relationships and trust are critical elements of selling services, and we need to show our prospects and clients that we care about their problems and want to help them find a solution. Having said that, you should resist offering solutions at this stage and instead say that you would like to go away and give the matter some thought before giving your recommendations. You could give some initial thoughts if you are being pressed, but make sure that your prospect is clear that is what they are.

Even though prospects often want to get answers quickly they will respect you more if you say you will go away and think about it. If you come up with answers too quickly there is the risk that they will think they are getting another client's solution.

You can imagine that it takes some effort to discover this information, and so this stage is really about asking questions and probing. The mistake a lot of novices make is that they spend all the precious time talking about their company and their services. They are selling too early and missing the opportunity to discover the information that will help to close the sale.

The test of whether you can move to the 'Propose Solution' stage of the consultative sales process is whether you have enough information to understand the issues and produce a proposal. One thing to bear in mind is that you do not have to take the sales opportunity to the next stage if you do not feel that there is a real sales opportunity for you or you do not think you would be able to provide a suitable solution. You will get more respect by being honest about it, and they may be more willing to talk to you about other problems if they believe that you will be straight with them. What's more, you will have saved yourself the work involved in producing a good proposal.

In most cases, however, it will be time to finish the discovery phase and start the phase of proposing a solution.

Propose Solution

By this stage you have all the information you need to be able to present a compelling solution and you are able to start putting together your 'pitch', which should be written. Even if you are going to present your solution face-to-face, you should have a written summary of the details. The reason is that your proposal is a sales document. It will contain some details of the proposed solution, but it must also sell your solution, too. This is because, despite all your best efforts, there will be some people—such as the finance director, perhaps—who you will not have managed to speak to, but who may get involved in the decision. For smaller businesses it could be a spouse, mentor, or accountant.

A written proposal not only covers the bases, but when done properly, is a good discipline to confirm understanding of the sale. Sometimes I am not totally sure where the return on investment will come from and it reveals itself when I'm writing out the proposal. The important thing to remember is that a proposal does not need to be a thick document. For smaller projects, it could be a one-page letter. What is crucial is to include various key pieces of information so that someone who has not been involved in the sales conversations can read it and see that it is a good deal. For more detailed proposals I recommend that there is a one-page executive summary that excludes the technical details and covers the essential points for making a decision.

We cover proposals in more depth in Chapter Seven, but for now the criteria for moving to the 'Negotiate Solution' stage is that the proposal has been delivered and acknowledged.

Negotiate Solution

Once you've proposed your solution, your prospects may have reservations and they will sometimes actually want to negotiate the makeup of the solution. For example, I recently gave a proposal to help a client set up a new sales team, which included liaising with the sales recruitment company and doing the first interviews on his behalf. Then I was to work with the sales person during the first 90 days to ensure they got off to a good start. This was due to his being very busy and also feeling that he was not a good judge as to whether someone could sell or not. By the time I had delivered the proposal, he had decided he wanted to give a family member a shot at the sales role and so the proposal needed to be reworked.

When I do a proposal I normally agree with the client that I will put forward a draft proposal and set expectations that we will shape (negotiate) the final proposal together. This allows me to suggest some optional extras. In some competitive situations it may not be possible to take this approach, but in many cases I co-create the final solution with the client. During this stage there could be what are commonly referred to in sales speak as 'objections', which I like to think of as 'reservations'. I rarely get objections due to price because of the way I manage the sales process, and I will explain this in Chapter Nine, along with offering some tips on negotiating.

If you are going to get any price objections, they will come out at this stage and it is important you prepare as to how you are going to handle them. If such objections come up regularly, you would be wise to look at the earlier stages of your sales process and identify what you can do to stop price objections from arising further down the line. They are often due to things like not qualifying the opportunity, talking about price too early, and not putting enough emphasis on the value the project will deliver.

If you do find that your client wants to negotiate a lower price, make sure, if at all possible, you do not drop your rates—and never do it without getting something in return that is worth at least as much to you. It is much better to put effort into deciding the rate in advance and then sticking to it.

When you are putting together your proposal you should be fairly clear as to what the client's next best alternative is. This could impact on pricing and even on your proposed solution. I remember one particular opportunity where I knew that I had a few competitors who would probably be offering similar solutions. I took the time to emphasise the benefits of working with me and explained exactly what was in it for them.

Many people needlessly give in to requests to lower costs, especially when confronted with professional buyers. I did so in my early days of sales, only to discover that the client would have paid the full price if I had kept my nerve. If you get to negotiating price, you can be pretty sure that the client wants to work with you and it is just down to 'horse trading'.

Ask for the Business

Closing the sale is something that people often find a bit tricky when they follow more traditional approaches to sales. If you approach the early stages of the consultative sales process correctly, you will understand how the decision will be made, and you are prepared to walk away from unsuitable opportunities that you do not think can be won. In these circumstances, closing the sale becomes more of a natural progression rather than a process in which you need to use pushy tactics.

This stage of the sales process is where a decision needs to be made, one way or another, and if you have covered all the bases earlier on in, this stage should be very quick and a bit of a formality.

Getting a 'No' is better than not knowing where you stand. The trick is to get your 'No's' early in the sales process, with good qualification. One thing I have learnt is that you will increase your chances of getting a 'Yes' by asking for the business, which can be as simple as saying:

"I would really like to work with you on this project, would you like to go ahead?"

Or

"I am looking forward to us working together, when would you like to get started?"

If the person starts coming back with issues and reservations, it is an indication that you are actually still at the 'Negotiate Solution' stage and more work needs to be done.

The criteria for leaving this stage are more than just getting a verbal 'Yes'. The sale is not closed until you have the appropriate documentation, such as a purchase order. For most of my services, I am paid in advance and so, for me, I know the sale is definitely closed when the cash is in the company bank account!

Deliver the Promise

This is the last stage of the consultative sales process, but if we do this important stage well, we will increase the chances of follow-on work, referrals, and testimonials. The follow-on work could be in the form of a project extension or it could be additional projects. It could even be internal recommendations for similar work with other parts of the same organisation. Delivering on your promises turns a sales process into a sales cycle, and after you have successfully delivered on a few projects, you will find that you may get multiple sales opportunities for new projects at the same time.

Hopefully, you can see that when you have delivered, or indeed exceeded your promises, you will start to be seen as a trusted adviser who not only has useful and reliable information and insights, but can also be trusted to deliver what they say they will.

Summary

In order to feel in control of sales and to be able to generate a regular flow of sales billable projects, it is important we understand the mechanics of sales and the various stages a sales opportunity needs to go through from an initial expression of interest to closing the sale. There are seven stages of the sales process:

1. Generate Interest
2. Qualify Interest
3. Discover Wants and Needs
4. Propose Solution
5. Negotiate Solution
6. Ask for the Business

7. Deliver the Promise

For each sales opportunity, we need to be clear what stage it is at and what we need to do to get it to the next stage. The process becomes a cycle leading to further new sales opportunities when you deliver your promises.

For free resources on **Consultative Selling for Professional Services**, including free mini-course, webinars, and e-books, visit **www.theaccidentalsalesman.com**

Chapter Three

Your 5-Star Clients

Introduction

One thing that makes sales much easier, especially for business developers who also need to do billable work, is to have a very clear sense of what constitutes an ideal client. When you have clarity as to who your ideal clients are, finding and winning business with them becomes so much easier. In this chapter we will define the top criteria for your ideal clients and how to use this information in the sales process.

Clients from Hell and how to avoid them

Julian was incredibly frustrated. His business was able to build incredibly complex websites using cutting edge technology and yet all his marketing effort seemed to attract clients with no money, no manners, and no idea what they wanted. It had been fun in the early years, but now he was finding business a bit of a chore. If only he could get more of the right kind of clients he would be making more money and his staff would stop complaining about rude clients.

Julian's problem is quite common. He did not have a clear sense of his ideal clients and their buying motivation, and as a result, his marketing messages were very generic. His website was designed to appeal to the masses, and when networking, he was quite unspecific. To make matters worse, he did not have any process to qualify and weed out unsuitable prospects; he was trying to win them all without realising that some would become 'Clients from Hell' and he would wish he'd never started working with them.

Once Julian had clarity with regard to his ideal clients, he was able to put out stronger marketing messages that were highly attractive to them and then use the 'Qualify Interest' stage of the consultative sales process to identify and eliminate the 'Clients from Hell'. As a consequence, he started winning clients who spent more money with his business and so were more profitable, and with whom his staff enjoyed working. He also avoided wasting huge amounts of time on unprofitable clients. His ideal clients also made sales easier for Julian by making referrals to their own clients and contacts.

Rate your prospects

Everywhere you go online these days you are asked to rate things. On TripAdvisor you rate hotels and accommodation, on Amazon you rate books and a lot more, and on eBay you rate suppliers. A common way to rate both things and people is to award them between one and five stars. The greater the number of stars awarded, the higher the approval rating. Whilst rating in this way is very subjective, it does help other people to gauge your opinions. What if you were able to rate your clients? Who would you give five stars to and who would get one star? Would any get no stars?

Whilst many people tell me that all their clients are important to them, if I ask them which specific client they like the best they will always have one or two that they prefer; and yet they are often unable to say just why they prefer them other than offering quite vague statements like, "They are nicer to deal with", or "They spend more money". We need something a little more objective. In the example above, the top five criteria for Julian's ideal clients at that time were:

★ They are located in London, England.

★ They have an entrepreneurial mindset.

★ They have sales of at least £0.5m.

★ Their workforce is based in multiple locations.

★ They are looking for cloud-based solutions.

I call these 5-Star Qualities, and when you have them defined, you can use them both in your qualification criteria and in making your marketing more targeted. When combined with what we will be covering in the next few chapters, your sales and marketing messages will also be much more attractive to your ideal clients and you will stand out from the crowd.

You can rate your prospects by giving them one star for each of the 5-Star Qualities. The ones with all five stars will be your 5-Star Prospects. If you have identified and listed your qualities correctly, then in my view, if they do not have any stars you should seriously consider qualifying out the opportunity. One star or more is okay, but normally you are looking for at least three stars. For Julian, three of the criteria became non-negotiable:

★ They have sales of at least £0.5m.

★ Their workforce is based in multiple locations.

★ They are looking for cloud-based solutions.

Rate your existing clients

In addition to rating your prospects, your 5-Star Qualities will help you to prioritise which of your existing clients you should be spending more time with in order to grow the business you do with them. Clients with five stars will be especially important for you to spend time with to explore new sales opportunities and referrals. You will also want to defend the account against competition in the best way possible—by strengthening the relationship and being seen as the trusted adviser.

If you have existing clients with zero stars, you may want to examine whether they are worth pursuing for any future business. If they are, then you may want to refine your 5-Star Qualities, as it would suggest that there is some adjustment to be made. At the very least you will probably want to do business development on a more reactive basis with that client, rather than investing prime business development time with them.

Defining your 5-Star Qualities

I would now like to lead you through a process for selecting your 5-Star Qualities and meeting your 5-Star Clients. We will do it in a number of logical steps. There will be exercises for you to do at each step, and in order to help you to fully understand the steps and apply the principle to your business, I thought it would be useful to give you a working example as we go through them, as that will make it more meaningful to you. Just for clarity, your list should not include a specific budget to do with the current opportunity, but it could well include a typical annual spend.

In this example, I will focus on an IT support client who came to me because they had certain sales that they were struggling to close. The first thing we needed to do was to get them to identify what made an ideal client. Coming straight out with your top five qualities is very difficult, so to get started, I recommend you first produce a 'laundry list'. Perhaps by getting together with your colleagues and having a brainstorming session.

Step 1: Brainstorm a list of the qualities of an ideal client

IT support example—Here is the initial list of qualities we produced in the order given:
1. The company needs to have between 15 and 100 PCs.
2. Head Office based in London and within the M25.

3. They need to collect payments by direct debit.
4. They value their time and know the cost of their down time.
5. They are not IT savvy and need 'hand-holding'.
6. They have someone responsible for IT (e.g. Finance Director).
7. They have old equipment.
8. They already have an IT support contract in place.
9. They have multiple sites.
10. They want a full-service (one-stop-shop).
11. They have fallen out with their IT Suppliers who have let them down.
12. Their prospects don't like being sold to by pushy sales people.
13. They have an entrepreneurial mindset.

Exercise
Get a piece of paper and write out a long list of all the different qualities you look for in an ideal client. Just keep listing at this stage rather than judging. You will get to do that next!

Step 2: Select the most important 5-Star Quality

From your long list now choose the one quality that is so important that without it you would not do business with a potential client.

IT Support Example
1. The company needs to have between 15 and 100 PCs.

47

Step 3: Select the rest of your 5-Star Qualities in order of importance

IT Support Example: Here are the 5-Star Qualities:
1. The company needs to have between 15 and 100 PCs.
2. Head Office based in London and within the M25.
3. They have fallen out with their IT Suppliers who have let them down.
4. They value their time and know the cost of their downtime.
5. They want a full-service (one-stop-shop).

Meet your 5-Star Clients

Now that you have your 5-Star Qualities, it's time for you to actually meet your existing 5-Star Clients and put names to them. Get a list of all your clients, ideally, in a spreadsheet. If you do not have many clients, you can add names of clients you have nearly won or those you would like to win. This is not as good, as you have not actually worked with them and they have not spent money with you; however, it is a start and it's better than having no focus. Now go through the list, line by line, and each time a client has one of the 5-Star Qualities, give them a star. When you have finished, each client on your list will have anything from zero stars to five stars against it. Your 5-Star Clients are the ones who have all five stars. It's as simple as that!

Exercise
Go through your client list and allocate a star for each of the 5-Star Qualities they have.

Now sort your list so that clients with five stars are at the top of the list and clients with zero stars are at the bottom. Write out your 5-Star Clients on a separate list. If do not have any with five Stars, that is okay. It is useful to know and it is exciting that you now know what to look for.

If you have clients on your list with no stars at all I would suggest that either you need to review your 5-Star Qualities or make a decision to not invest any more sales and marketing activity in winning that type of client. Indeed, you should be focusing your sales and marketing activity on your 5-Star Clients. You will inevitably get people who respond who do not have all five stars, but I would be cautious of taking on a client who does not merit any stars.

You may also find that your 5-Star Clients are not the ones that currently produce the most sales. This is not a problem. During the course of this book you will learn how you can earn significantly more money from your 5-Star Clients by focusing on finding additional problems you can solve for them or providing a fuller solution to what you currently offer.

You should just sense-check the list by making sure that all the clients on it are the type of client you would like to attract and also would like to be doing even more business with. If there are any on the list that should not be there, you will need to review and fine tune your 5-Star Qualities and redo the exercise.

Exercise
Create a prioritised list of clients based on the number of stars awarded and meet your 5-Star Clients! Do a quick sense-check to make sure these are the clients you would most like to attract and win.

What to do when you don't yet have any paying clients

Whilst the ultimate test for 5-Star Clients is them paying cash for your services, there are lots of clues as to who could be your 5-Star Clients. For example, do you have specialist knowledge or experience in a particular industry? Does your business serve people with a problem like you once had? If you have been working with clients who should have been able to afford to pay but have not done so to date, it could just be related to your inexperience at making a sales approach or that perhaps you have not yet felt comfortable charging but intend to do so.

When I am working with start-up companies I get them to tell me their story of how they started in business, why they started in business, and what they were doing before. There are always clues which will point to who would make an ideal client. You do have to be able to see things in terms of how the client will benefit. Your story could reveal some clues as to what would make an ideal client for where you are now in your business. It may change in the future as your business grows, but it is important that you start with your current situation and recent past.

What to do if you do not yet have any 5-Star Clients

One of the benefits of meeting your 5-Star Clients is that you can start to identify with those types of clients. They will be a great source of stories that will help you with your marketing and sales processes, as you will see in later chapters.

If you do not yet have any 5-Star Clients, you may want to add to your list what I call 'near misses'. These are sales that you wanted to win, and should have won, but narrowly missed out on. Check to see if any of those fit your 5-Star criteria and then look at the reasons why you lost the sale. If you did not get that information from your prospect at the time, then consider going back to them and asking. What were the main objections? If it was anything to do with price or issues that can be overcome with better selling skills, then add them to your list of 5-Star Clients. If it was something structural, like they were looking for an international presence and you cannot currently provide that, then you should go back and check your 5-Star Qualities to see if you need to make any changes.

Just to be clear, we are looking to identify examples of 5-Star Clients so you can get more of them, rather than adding these near misses to your actual clients list. It's all about gaining clarity with regard to the type(s) of clients you should be aiming for.

If you have a lot of clients with 4-Star Qualities, look to see if there is any consistency with regard to the missing star. If there is, it could be that you need to change things so that you will be more appealing to clients with that quality or it could mean you need to review your 5-Star Qualities. If there is no consistency with regard to the missing star, my recommendation is to proceed with the rest of the book based on your 4-Star Clients. It is probably just a matter of time before you acquire 5-Star Clients and when you apply the insights of the book, you will be more likely to speed up the process of finding clients with all 5-Star Qualities.

If you have only 3-Star Clients or less, and you have a good number of clients, then review your 5-Star Qualities and make sure you are happy with them. If you still have only clients with three stars or less, it just means we will need to be more creative when it comes to being able to answer the 'why you?' question that we will cover in the next chapter.

Summary

In this chapter we went through the process of meeting your 5-Star Clients. We identified the five most important qualities that clients require to qualify as an ideal client. We then went through your client list and allocated a star for each of the qualities your clients possess and we prioritised them according to the number of stars they have. The clients possessing all five stars are your 5-Star Clients, and now you know them by name!

> For free resources on **Consultative Selling for Professional Services**, including free mini-course, webinars, and e-books, visit **www.theaccidentalsalesman.com**

Chapter Four

The 'Why' Factor

Introduction

In Chapter One we have seen the importance of buying motivation in sales, and in this chapter we are going to delve much deeper into the subject. Now that you know who your 5-Star Clients are, we need to discover their different buying motives. We will also discover why your 5-Star Clients will want to buy from you and not your competitors. Gaining these insights will make it easier to generate more interest from existing and potential 5-Star Clients and it will make it easier to win the sale.

There are many reasons why people buy

One of the biggest insights I got into sales was that people can be motivated to buy a specific product or service for a number of possible reasons rather than there just being one single reason. Moreover, that motivation is totally different as to why they decide to buy from us and not our competitors. In addition, the motivation to continue to buy from us may be different from the motivation to make the first purchase. Like many people, I used to assume that the reason my best clients bought from me was the quality of service and the relationship. Whilst it was true, that would only be attractive to people who wanted a better level of service. Moreover, there are few service companies that do not claim to offer a superior level of service, and the fact of the matter is that it is all very subjective.

If we want to attract more 5-Star Clients and get them to start to buy from us, we need to understand what originally motivated our existing 5-Star Clients to seek a supplier of our services—then we can find other businesses that currently have similar motivations. From my research of working with almost a thousand small and medium-sized service businesses, I have discovered that, rather than just one, there are normally five or six different buying motivations for any value proposition. Different companies have different reasons for being interested in buying our services, and we want to find the one that is the best fit with what we offer.

Knowing why they buy is important in order to attract them to us. Then, once they have decided what they are buying, we need to know why they would buy from us and not from one of our competitors.

In other words, we need to discover:

- Why do our 5-Star Clients start buying?
- Why do our 5-Star Clients decide to buy from us?

These are two very different buying motives and each impacts different stages of the sales process. To generate buying interest from a 5-Star Client we need, through our communication, to appeal to their primary reason for buying a particular proposition. *To get them to decide to buy from us so that we win the sale is a completely different matter, and it is important that we are clear about the difference.* We also need to be clear about when, during the sales process, we address each of these two buying motivations.

If your 5-Star Clients are educated buyers of your services, then telling them about how you are different from your competitors may be important at the 'Generate Interest' stage. For most of us, however, it is much easier to engage prospects in a sales conversation by appealing to their primary buying motivation.

A practical example

One of the stories I use to help people understand the concept of *buying motivation* is the work I did with an international sewing machine company. I tell this story because it is a simple illustration of *buying motivation* with something very tangible. I find that once people understand the concepts using this simple example, it is easy for them to apply the principles to more complex professional services.

The marketing manager of this sewing machine company was organising a conference for their resellers and wanted me to be their keynote speaker. He was worried about the impact the Internet was having on the sales coming from resellers, and he wanted me to help them win more local business from people walking into their stores, rather than them relying on the Internet.

The resellers are all small and medium-sized businesses that typically own one or more high street stores selling sewing machines, haberdashery, and services such as training and servicing. The impact of people buying their sewing machines online was driving a lot of resellers out of business. People were researching sewing machines online in the first instance, then they would go into a local store to look at the sewing machine and ask the people in the shop questions, then they would go back home and buy it online—a practice known as 'showrooming'.

This buyer activity was leading to the resellers competing with each another online based on price, and as a result they were not making much money. Many resellers had to move away from the high street into cheaper premises, which meant they were also missing out on any passing trade. The marketing manager could see that the resellers' lack of selling skill was threatening the whole existence of their reseller network. They wanted me to show them how they could get people coming into their store, not only to buy whilst they were in the store, but also to pay a higher price than buying exactly the same machine online.

I proposed that my keynote speech should focus on helping them understand the buying motivations of people entering the shop and how to use value-added services to increase the perceived value of buying their sewing machine locally. The marketing manager told me that their ideal clients were locally based women, aged 45 to 55 years old, who are interested in sewing and embroidery. When I asked him why they wanted to buy a sewing machine in the first place, his only answer was that they wanted to do things like make curtains, make clothes, repair clothes, and make crafts.

Client Archetypes

I have developed a technique I call 'Client Archetypes' to help businesses quickly distinguish different buying motivations for a particular service. It basically involves identifying different primary buying motivations and giving them a name. There are normally five or six Client Archetypes for any product or service, and in the case of the sewing machine company, I managed to come up with five. I am going to go through these five Client Archetypes with you, and as you read through the descriptions I would like you to start thinking what the Client Archetypes for your services might look like.

An important aspect of Client Archetypes is the name we associate with each buying motive. It should be one or two words that sum up the buying motivation. Once you have done this for your business you should be able to list specific clients against each Client Archetype. This will then make it easier to understand with whom we are communicating, what questions to ask, and what they will find attractive.

The five Client Archetypes for this sewing machine company are:

- The Money-savers
- The Fashionistas
- The Crafties
- The Part-time Entrepreneurs
- The Professionals

The Money-savers

Money-savers, as the name suggests, are interested in saving money. Not just saving money on the sewing machine, but also saving money *with* the sewing machine. Their primary buying motivation for walking in the store was because they wanted to save money by making things like curtains, soft furnishings and clothes. They wanted the sewing machine as a means of saving money rather than having to buy those things ready-made. As a Money-saver, their whole mindset when buying a sewing machine was to save money, and of course, they would also want to spend as little as possible on the sewing machine. They would potentially be interested in reconditioned sewing machines if the store was able to sell them.

The Fashionistas

Whilst the Fashionistas would probably like to get a sewing machine at the lowest price, that is not their *primary buying motivation*. The Fashionistas love fashion and clothes. They want to look stylish, and their primary motivation for buying a sewing machine is to look good. They want to make their own clothes and make alterations to clothes. Their buying behaviour is being driven by the desire to make their own clothes in order to look fashionable. Fashionistas may be interested in attending local workshops where they can learn dressmaking skills and how to design their own clothes. They may also be interested in meeting other Fashionistas and swapping ideas and patterns. A local store could use this to attract Fashionistas to the store and give them a reason to buy the sewing machine from them rather than buying it online.

The Crafties

Crafties are interested in buying a sewing machine for a completely different reason: they like to make things like crafts as a creative outlet. They probably have a desk job and make things as a hobby. The thing about Crafties is that they are always thinking of their next project and trying new things. Perhaps they are currently doing a cross-stitch pattern and thinking about a project that requires a sewing machine. So the primary buying motivation for the Crafties is to use a sewing machine for their hobby of making crafts. I could have named them the Hobbyists, but at the time I felt Crafties would be more memorable.

As Crafties are always looking to do new things, they might be interested in workshops and training in sewing and embroidery techniques. They might also like to meet and share ideas with other local Crafties. The resellers could probably use the training events to get them interested in more sophisticated machines, and I suggested they may want to consider introducing a part-exchange policy, meaning they could then sell the reconditioned sewing machines to the Money-savers. Again, you can see that if you made these events exclusive to Crafties, they'd have good potential reasons for buying locally rather than on the Internet.

The Part-time Entrepreneurs

This group of people is motivated to buy a sewing machine so that they can make money in their spare time. Just like the other Client Archetypes, they may use their sewing machine to make curtains, clothes, soft furnishings, and crafts, but their motivation to do so is to earn extra money. Their reason for buying local would be servicing. If their sewing machine was to break down they would not be able to use it to make money. It would be far more convenient to be able to drop their sewing machine into their local store rather than having to post it to another part of the country.

The Professionals

This group is similar to the Part-time Entrepreneurs, but their primary motivation for buying a sewing machine is to use it to earn a full-time living. As a consequence, they would need a fast turnaround on servicing because it would affect their ability to earn their living. All the more reason for buying local.

Summary

I hope you can see that for every Client Archetype except the Money-savers, there is a good reason for the resellers to use to get people to buy locally rather than go for the lowest price on the Internet. From a sales perspective, they were advised to spend as little time as possible with the Money-savers as there would be a high probability that no matter what was said they would still go for the lowest price they could pay.

ARCHETYPE	PRIMARY MOTIVATOR
Money-savers	Save money by making things
Fashionistas	Make their own stylish clothes
Crafties	Creative outlet
Part-time Entrepreneurs	Earn extra money
Professionals	Earn a living

IT Services Example

Here are the Client Archetypes for the IT services company I featured in the previous chapter:

ARCHETYPE	PRIMARY MOTIVATOR
Annoyed	Their IT support company has let them down and they are looking for an alternative supplier.
Upgraders	They are looking for a fuller service than their current IT support company is able to provide.
Problem Solvers	They have a problem that has been ongoing and which their existing support company has not been able to fix.
Buyers	They are looking for a particular type of software or service not supplied by their existing IT support company; for example, second line support.
Advice Seekers	They are seeking advice on an issue, and they have not had a satisfactory answer from their existing IT support company.
Comparers	They are looking to reduce the cost of their IT support, and they are checking the market to see how their existing IT support company compares.

Notes:

There is a natural inertia towards making change. The top three Client Archetypes are likely to have the strongest motivation or potential motivation to change their providers of IT support. At the very least it will be enough motivation to enable the IT support company to provide a product or service as a stepping stone towards selling an IT support contract.

Annoyed

This will be the strongest motivation. Find out more about why they are annoyed and what impact that has had on the business. Also ask whether it was a one off or if it is likely to happen again in the future. You want them to tell you that they have lost confidence in their current IT support company.

Upgraders

The company is probably growing and they have outgrown their current IT support company, who is unable to give them the attention and support they now need. They want a 'one stop shop' and a much more responsive support. They are probably taking a more cool-headed and cautious approach to selecting their IT support company than the Annoyed.

Problem Solvers

The buying motivation will be driven by the desire to solve a specific problem rather than thinking about switching suppliers. The fact that their existing IT support company has not been able to solve the problem does open the door to potentially win the contract on renewal—if they can solve the problem and nurture the relationship.

Buyers

Find out why the prospect wants to buy the product or service and focus on that sale, whilst finding out as much as possible about their existing IT support arrangements for any future sales pitch. If there is something that should be offered as standard (for example back up or telephone support), then follow a similar strategy to the one you'd use for the Problem Solvers Client Archetype.

Advice Seekers

This IT services supply company attracts quite a few people who have an existing IT services contract and whose primary interest when making contact is to get some free advice. The danger is that these people may have no current desire to change their IT services company and a lot of time could be wasted on them. However, with the right questioning, it could be possible to turn an Advice Seeker into an Upgrader. If they are the right profile of client, but only currently looking for advice, then it could be worth giving the advice and nurturing the relationship until they are ready to buy something specific or talk about changing their IT support company. Knowing that they are an Advice Seeker will mean that you can respond appropriately.

Comparers

The primary buying motivation is driven by the desire to save money. We could have called them the Money-savers, but my client felt that Comparers was a better fit for them. It is important to understand from a prospect why they are comparing the market and whether there are any service issues with their current supplier. The danger is that they are just trying to get competitors to quote lower prices so that they can negotiate a lower price with their existing supplier. People rarely change service providers based on price alone because, unlike products, humans are not identical. Switching from the status quo is a big risk and there normally needs to be another reason as well as price. If you offer an IT audit you could potentially uncover problems that could change the nature of the conversation to an Upgrader, but given the high service levels this IT services company provide, I would not advise selling on price.

Although it's not always possible, in this case the buying motivations for the top two Client Archetypes were related, and we were able to share a similar message about the IT Support company's higher levels of responsiveness and proactive approach to IT support.

It is worth noting that these Client Archetypes are specific to this particular IT Support company even though other IT support companies may recognize similar buying motivations. We could also do a Client Archetype exercise on other areas of their business, such as telephony and bespoke software development.

Primary buying motivation

A final point to note about primary motivation is that it is not the **only** motivation a client or potential client has when buying. It is the one that is **most** important to them. Going back to the sewing machine example, you can take it for granted that almost every customer wanted to pay the lowest price possible. Some, however, would pay extra and buy locally so that they could get access to the local classes and networking events where they could learn and exchange ideas—provided that this was made exclusive to customers.

Discovering why *your* 5-Star Clients buy

Now it is your turn to discover the primary motivators for your 5-Star Clients and give them each a Client Archetype name.

EXERCISE ONE
Against each of your 5-Star Clients write the primary motivation for them making contact and expressing an interest. If you have less than five primary motivators or you don't yet have any 5-Star Clients, then work down the other clients on your list. Otherwise, just think about why someone might be interested in talking to you about your services.

EXERCISE TWO
Now turn each of the primary motivators into a Client Archetype by giving them a name.

EXERCISE THREE
Prioritise your list of Client Archetypes, putting the strongest buying motivation at the top.

Why they buy from you and no one else

In the Internet age it has never been easier to find alternative suppliers to meet almost any need. It is also very telling how similar many businesses seem to be to their competitors. Services are becoming commodities. If you want to stand out from the crowd and you want to charge premium rates for your services, then you need to be different. Whilst having a point of difference for the whole range of services you offer may be a struggle, it is quite easy to have a significant point of difference for the *first* service you sell to your 5-Star Clients if you focus on your area of maximum credibility. Once you have used the primary sale to become a trusted adviser to a client, then you will find the need to be dramatically different is reduced, too. The trusted adviser status will increasingly become your competitive advantage. However, to win the account in the first place you do need to be different from your competitors, especially if your prospective client is already working with a competitor.

Be a specialist

If you needed brain surgery, who would you rather have do the operation:

    a. A specialist, who only does brain surgery? or

    b. A generalist, who occasionally does brain surgery?

Would you be prepared to pay more for a specialist? I am confident that you would. When something is important to get right we want to make sure we get results the first time. This is a massive difference between products and services. We can test a product before we buy, and normally a product will have predictable results. The trouble with services is that they typically involve humans, and we cannot be sure of the results we are going to get.

If you can show your target audience that you have specialist experience that is relevant to them, it could give them more comfort when choosing you over their other alternatives, including doing it themselves and not doing anything at all.

My recommendation is for you to specialise in your area of **maximum credibility** and focus on specialisation for your first sale; then, once you have delivered on your promises and won the trust of your client, you will be able to more easily sell services where there is less difference between what you offer compared to what your competitors offer.

A good example of how you can use specialisation to gain a competitive edge is one of my first clients. Before setting up a meeting effectiveness consultancy, he had been a senior buyer for a major supermarket in the UK. He had been in business for six months and was struggling to get any interest. He was very knowledgeable about meetings, but he had no success stories to point to. In short, he could not prove that he could deliver what he promised, and despite lots of discussions with former suppliers to the supermarket who he knew really well, he was not winning any business.

His fortunes changed when we changed the focus to his area of maximum credibility. He told me about the requests he was getting from his former supermarket supplier contacts for advice as to how they could win more business with the supermarket. They were not interested in general meeting advice, but they were very interested in being more effective in having sales meetings with the supermarket chain. This was an area of massive credibility, especially as many of those contacts had tried to sell more products to him in the past without success.

By framing his service in terms of where he has maximum credibility and targeting companies with a compelling motivation to buy he was able to transform the nature of the sales conversations. Within three months his business was transformed, and he had to start taking on associates and employing people. In addition, once he had won the initial work based around effective buyer meetings, he was able to generate interest in his other meeting services.

I find that most professional services businesses have at least one area of maximum credibility, and often it is revealed through the story of how and why the business or a particular service arose in the first place. Finding that specialisation and having the confidence to use it will make a massive difference in answering the "why you?" question, because people like to know they are working with a specialist.

Here are some examples of potential specialisation:

- Ultra-high levels of responsiveness.

- Solving extremely technically challenging problems.

- Working in a very specific part of an industry when domain knowledge is important.

- Working with a specialist product.

- Working on international projects.

Specialising in nothing

The point about being a specialist is about building credibility. You can often get an edge over generalists and command higher rates where the buying motivation is strong enough. I see many businesses that refuse to really specialise and yet claim to be specialists in a long list of areas. This can actually damage credibility as it shows that you are just trying to appear to be different when in actual fact you are just a generalist. I believe it is possible to have more than one specialist area, but I would keep it to as few as possible. The important thing is to make sure your specialisation is attractive to your 5-Star Clients and gives you an edge over your competitors in winning your first piece of work. Once you are tried, tested, and trusted you will often be able to win work over a specialist, but you must first develop a track record of delivering results.

Aim to be a hyper-specialist

Being a specialist is better than being a generalist, but if the benefits of your specialisation are not apparent then it will not help you win business. For example, you may specialise in a particular product, but if there are hundreds of other companies that specialise in that product too, then there will need to be some other reason for choosing your business rather than your hundreds of direct competitors.

Working in the charity sector would be a specialist area. Working with mental health charities would be a hyper-specialist area.

In our IT services example, they realised that although their fast response times were impressive, there were lots of competitors also offering the same. One thing that was different was their offering second line support for bespoke software, which for their target audience was a particular requirement and actually a reason why many of their 5-Star Clients first started talking to them.

Here are some more examples of hyper-specialisms:

Specialism	Hyper-Specialism
Business intelligence consulting	Data quality consulting
Bespoke software development	Bespoke software development for accountants
Website testing	Website testing on mobile devices
IT support for small businesses	Secure backup for independent financial advisers (IFAs)
Website development	Websites for wine wholesalers

EXERCISE
Go through your client list and think about what services you have provided for them to see if there are any obvious areas of hyper-specialism or reasons why your 5-Star Clients would choose to work with you over your competitors—at least for a specific service.

Prove it!

Credibility is an important part of the sales process, especially once you have presented your solution and you are hoping to get your proposal approved. A prospect may happily speak to you up to that point, but when it comes to making a decision, they tend to play safe, especially where there are large sums of money involved, or in the case of corporates, their own personal credibility is on the line. People in companies do not like taking risks, and given the choice of two or more options, they will almost always play it safe. You need to expect to have to prove your expertise by providing a contact to an existing client as a reference. This is normally just on the first sale, and if you focus on your area of maximum credibility it should be easy to do. You can give testimonials and case studies, but without names they are worthless, and if you include names you need to expect that someone may call them!

This may seem tedious, but once you have proven your expertise, you will have given your prospective 5-Star Client comfort that they are in safe hands. And when you deliver on your promise, you will be well on your way to becoming a trusted adviser. You will find you will win against competitors even if there are no real differences in your services. Furthermore, when you tailor your services specifically to the buying motivations of your 5-Star Clients, you will find you start to put blue water between your company and your nearest competitors because you give your clients peace of mind.

Summary

When you understand why your 5-Star Clients buy from you it makes it easier to both attract and win more of them. Why they start to talk to you will be driven by their buying motivation. When we understand what motivates a 5-Star Client to want to talk to us, we can communicate messages that tap into that buying motivation and initiate the first stage of the sales process: 'Generate Interest'.

There are normally five or six different motivators for any service proposition, and we did an exercise called Client Archetypes where we identified the primary buying motivations and gave them a name. Whilst the buying motivation will get a sales conversation started, there needs to be a reason why your potential new client will buy from you rather than your competition. Once you are seen as a trusted adviser you will be at a competitive advantage, but until then your best strategy is likely to focus your first sale on an area where you have demonstrable specialist expertise that makes you a safe choice.

You do need to be prepared to prove that you have the technical expertise that you claim, especially when working with larger companies who tend to play safe and take more care over buying decisions.

> For free resources on **Consultative Selling for Professional Services**, including free mini-course, webinars, and e-books, visit **www.theaccidentalsalesman.com**

Chapter Five

Start Small and Grow

Introduction

Many small and medium-sized consulting firms have one or two very large client accounts. These client accounts will have probably began as a small account and grown over time. As the consultancy grows they often try to win larger projects, and they end up spending a lot of time and effort trying to win against stiff competition. People in larger companies like to play it safe, and until you are tried, tested, and trusted in winning large projects—especially against big consulting firms—it is a challenge. With larger projects, your prospects will tend to go with the low-risk option and use an existing supplier they trust, or a major brand, even if it means paying more. In this chapter I will show you how to use this aspect of human nature to your advantage so that you are able to make sales easier for yourself, and over time, build very large client accounts.

Think big but start small

The temptation in sales is to make the sale as big as possible. The problem is that when you make your first sale you are not tried, tested, and trusted. Being recommended by a trusted contact helps, and so does being able to allow the prospect to speak to some of your existing clients. However, when it comes to the crunch, the fear of taking risks means that unless you are working for a major consulting brand or you have proven specialist experience, you will probably be in a weak competitive position.

Yet once you become a trusted adviser, winning large projects against major brands will be much easier and often projects will be awarded without having to compete at all! I remember in my IT consulting days I helped a major police force to write a bid document, knowing that it was our project to lose. The other companies competing did not really stand much chance of winning. If you are bidding for large projects, you should be wondering who is helping them write the request for proposal.

Let's look at it from your prospect's perspective. Imagine you have a very important delivery to make. It absolutely has to arrive on time or there will be serious consequences. You can use your usual supplier, who has never let you down, but is very expensive, or a local company you have been introduced to who looks very impressive and is significantly cheaper. You want to start saving money, but the time to test a new company out is not when it really matters. You would probably give them some smaller jobs first to see how reliable they are before trusting them with a career defining assignment. The same happens with professional services. A potential client will want to test you out before handing over a very large project. So my recommendation is to make it easy for them to do so by always starting off with a small sale.

Primary sale, subsequent sale

Not only should the first sale be relatively small, it should be addressing an unresolved problem that your prospective client has. Trying to compete by offering the same services as your competitors is hard work. If they have already worked with a competitor, there is the risk that after all your hard work in getting them interested, they will end up buying the service from the competitor. It is much easier to win work in a highly focused specialist area. Once you have won your first project you now have a bridgehead to start winning more work, even though the client might have a working relationship with a competitor. Your area of specialisation should make you an obvious choice, and that is why I advise clients to use that specialism strategically to win the first sale.

Example 1

A small and growing plastics company is based in the UK, with a factory in Eastern Europe. The IT infrastructure in both locations is nice and stable and the company is doing well. The company is building a sales team in both locations, and there is a need to make changes to their bespoke quoting software and to also install a new CRM module to their accounting software. Although the IT support company is very good at resolving support calls, they have been dragging their feet over installing the software and do not seem to want to get involved in supporting the quoting software. The plastics company is in the middle of a contract and is also happy with the general support they receive. All they want is to get some changes made and get a package installed.

Without success, an IT support client had been targeting this company to win their general support contact each time it came up for renewal. We identified that supporting bespoke software was a major point of difference and an area of maximum credibility. Rather than waiting for the time when the IT support contract would be renewed, they seized the opportunity to win the small piece of work. They did a great job and spent time nurturing the relationship. Within six months they had won the entire support contract of both the UK and the site in Eastern Europe. They then went on to strategically use unsupported bespoke software as a way of breaking into other accounts which already had an existing supplier.

Example 2

The finance department of an airline uses a particular business intelligence tool for planning and forecasting, as well as management reporting. The software company sold the system direct and it is performing well. The finance director gets a consultant from the software company to come in and make changes to the system. The airline is part of a very large tour operator and they are big customers of the software company. They use many of their different software packages and buy a lot of consulting services, too. Indeed, the IT director used to work for the software company and has an excellent relationship with his account manager.

The finance department is always very busy, and the finance director is getting frustrated because one of his finance managers is supposed to be developing a cash flow forecast system and it does not seem to be progressing. The finance director has dropped a few hints to the consultant, but he is a product specialist rather than someone who fully understands finance.

A relatively small IT consultancy that worked with the software and specialised in hiring qualified accountants was able to win a small project to develop the cash flow forecast system. Then, through doing a good job and working on the relationship, they won more and more work away from the software company. The airline ended up spending over £100,000 per year in consulting revenues even though their client remained loyal to the software company.

EXERCISE
Consider what would make an ideal primary sale for your business. Make sure it is an area where you have specialist expertise.

Designing growth into your sales process

It takes a fair amount of time and effort to win new clients, and so it is better to find clients that are able to produce project work on an ongoing basis. Indeed, a 5-Star Client should be one that keeps coming back for more and more services. If you focus on winning 5-Star Clients and make sure you take care of them in the early days, they will see you as a trusted adviser and make sales very easy for you to achieve. They will not only contact you when they want to talk through a potential project, they will recommend you to colleagues and contacts. I remember the biggest single sale I made when I was building my IT consulting practice arose as a result of an internal recommendation. There was no competition! This was a common feature in the second and third year of a relationship because of the hard work I had put into building the relationship in the first year.

Since it is important to start small and grow, we should design this into our client acquisition strategy. We should focus our marketing and lead generation activity on attracting potential 5-Star Clients with specific buying motivations and then have a standard first sale which we use to start each client off with. This is not because we are incapable of making a large sale; it's because we want to give our new client the opportunity to feel comfortable working with us without taking a large risk. Although it is not guaranteed, we should then expect to make a follow-on sale to a good proportion of our clients.

It is not necessary to start every project with a small sale, just the very first project. Once we are well established within a client account we should then be in a good competitive position. You may decide to strategically start small with some projects with existing clients to get some momentum. For example, doing a small initial pilot project will help get the project started and minimise the risk. Once people can see that it is going to be a success they can then expand the project with confidence.

Different ways to grow a client account

There are three major ways to grow a client account on a proactive basis:

- Project expansions
- New projects
- Client expansion

Project expansions

In classic sales terminology, a project expansion is known as upselling. You start off with a small sale and then seek to expand the project once you have shown initial success. Your small primary sale should be designed to be capable of expanding a project. For example, a health check or audit will often find problems, and any one of those problems could lead to a project expansion. My advice is to design the deliverable of the small first sale so that it does not guarantee a project expansion. Normally, you would sell it on the basis that they can use the information to do the work internally or with an alternative supplier. However, if you do a great job and you are working in your specialist area, there is a good chance that you will get the follow-on work. If it is obvious that the health-check is just a vehicle for you to write a proposal it will take a lot more effort to get a client to be prepared to pay for the first sale. I prefer to make the first sale an independent service product that has high-perceived value. The prospect of the client being able to do the work themselves makes it appealing, and it makes it seem much more independent and unbiased.

New projects

A healthy way of growing a client account is by finding additional projects with your existing client contact. Whilst working at a client's premises on consulting work, you can see opportunities everywhere if you know what to look and listen out for. Having done the work on Client Archetypes and buying motivation for your different propositions, you will be able to recognise the problems you are able to fix. The trick is to start a conversation with the client about the problem; we will be covering how to do this in the next chapter.

You will make it easier to talk about additional projects if you design regular account reviews into your way of doing business. During the account review, you will both review the delivery of the service since the last review and confirm actions. You will then look forward to the next period and identify what needs to happen. It's during the conversation about the forthcoming period that you can discuss other problems. If you are providing ongoing services like IT Support, you can schedule a review every three months. If you are doing a project like a software development, you will include regular reviews during the life of the project, with a formal review once the project has been completed. It will be much easier to gain agreement if you tell your new client that this is how you do business. It will make you look more professional, and even though there will be a time cost, you should see it as part of your business development activity.

Client expansion

If you really want to build a client account and make sales easy for yourself, you should be looking to expand your client accounts beyond your current client contacts. To do this you need to network within your client account, developing relationships as you go. You can use your trusted relationship with your existing client contacts to get introduced to new client contacts that might require similar services. For example, say you have been engaged to provide services to a company which is a subsidiary of a large group. You can ask your client contact to introduce you to their counterpart in one or more of the sister companies. It's the same as a referral, except that it's an internal referral and therefore much easier to ask for. Also, the fact that you have done some great work within the same company will make it an internal reference site. Your client contacts will become your champions.

EXERCISE
Review your existing client accounts one-by-one and consider the growth potential for project expansion, new projects, and client expansion.

Prioritising accounts for growth

As business developers, we want to build our accounts but we have a limited time available, especially if we have responsibilities for delivering billable work. Some of our clients will have much bigger scope for sales growth than others, and the challenge is to know where best to spend our limited business development time. A big mistake is to spend all of our business development time with our largest accounts just because they are large. Whilst they are no doubt important and we need to defend our most important accounts against competition, we should be allocating sufficient business development time on accounts where there is good growth potential. Our 5-Star Clients should be the ones where there is the most business growth potential, although some will have more scope for growth than others.

Rocks, pebbles, and sand

In his excellent book, *The 7 Habits Of Highly Effective People*, Stephen Covey uses the analogy of putting rocks, pebbles, and sand into a beer glass. The habit is called 'Put first things first' and it is about becoming more effective with your time management. I recommend reading the book to get the full value, but the essence of the analogy is that you will be able to get more rocks, pebbles, and sand into a beer glass if you put the rocks in first, then the pebbles, and finally the sand. This is because the pebbles will fit into the spaces between the rocks and the sand will fill up the remaining space. Try doing it the other way around and the sand takes up a lot of space, leaving insufficient room for the rocks. In his book, Stephen Covey is using the rocks to symbolise tasks. The rocks are the most important tasks, and he suggests we focus on these first, then fit other tasks around them.

The same applies to client account development. The rocks are the clients with the biggest revenue potential. They tend to take a lot more time and effort to win and are worth the effort because of their potential for sales growth. However, if we only sought rock accounts we might not get our required sales results fast enough. At the other extreme, sand client accounts are quite easy to win in comparison, but the sales growth potential is limited. If we spent our time focused just on winning sand client accounts, we would make a fast start but our sales would plateau because of the limited growth potential of sand client accounts. We would be spending all our time winning clients and not on growing them. Apart from being hard work, especially if we have the need to deliver client work, it will lead to much lower sales overall.

The answer is to take a leaf out of Steven Covey's book and focus your business development activity around winning and developing the rocks. At the same time you seek to win and grow both pebble and sand client accounts. (Pebbles are halfway between sand and rocks.) A portfolio of all three will mean you balance short-term and longer-term needs. Whilst you might travel for several hours for a sales meeting with a potential rock, you would not do so for a potential sand account. However, when you are travelling for a meeting with a potential rock client account, you might also seek to fit in some visits in the same area with pebble and sand type clients and prospects.

Defining your rock, pebble, and sand client accounts

You may want to call your different categories of client account something different to rock, pebble, and sand. Many businesses refer to them instead as gold, silver, and bronze accounts to denote their value to the business. Whatever you decide to call them, you must not make the common mistake of classifying them based on existing revenue. If you do that, you might not pay attention to accounts that do not currently yield a lot of existing revenue, but which with some focused activity, would grow into major client accounts. My recommendation is to assess the annual sales potential over the next two or three years and then have bands of annual sales revenue for each. For example:

Client type	Minimum potential annual revenue
Rock	£250,000
Pebble	£100,000
Sand	£50,000

Using the example above, the way this works is that you would not target any company that did not have the capacity to spend at least £50,000 a year on your company's services. Extending this example, which of the following two sales enquiries would you go for, and which one would you qualify out?

Opportunity 1

You get an enquiry for a one-off project worth £40,000, with little scope for any follow-on work.

Opportunity 2

You get an enquiry for a small project you estimate to be worth £500, with the prospect of plenty of follow-on work which you estimate could be worth at least £75,000 a year. It could take a couple of years to reach its full potential.

If it was me and I had a choice, I would go for the second opportunity and I'd be very excited about it, even though it was currently just a small project. I would give it my all, because I would want the full £75,000. The first opportunity would be below the threshold of my minimum client size and so I would not pursue it. Assuming I did not have an existing relationship with them, I would be at a competitive disadvantage, and the lack of potential follow-on work would mean that I would not be making the best use of my business development time. My aim is to create client accounts that grow over time and allow me to both deliver paid consultancy and also work on finding project work for myself and my team.

Assessing potential

It is not easy to assess the potential of a client account as you can always increase potential by adding new services that you can offer to existing clients. It is very much down to the fit between the client organisation and your organisation. A good place to start is with your 5-Star Clients. If you have correctly graded your clients and prospects, then the ones with five stars should naturally have more potential than those with one star. The fit between your two organisations is important, and it is possible that your 5-Star Clients do not see you as five star a supplier! That is all down to fine-tuning your 5-Star Qualities.

Having said that, when it comes to assessing potential there are a number of clues we can use, such as the current or predicted capacity for spending on your type of services. For example, if you are in the business of providing mergers and acquisitions consultancy, then a small but fast growing company could have much bigger potential over time than a large corporate who is already dominant and who historically has gone for organic growth. You never can tell exactly, so it is hard to do it scientifically, but what we can do is use our knowledge of our clients to see where there is a good fit between their anticipated future needs and the value we can add. We need to periodically review the situation, too, as changes within a client account can change the potential quite dramatically. For example, if your company provides specialist consulting around a particular software platform and the client decides to switch to a different software platform, then your potential revenues can change quite significantly.

EXERCISE
Decide on the potential revenue bands for Rock, Pebble, and Sand accounts. Go through your client list and identify those that fall within those revenue bands.

81

Defending your client accounts

Just as you can start small to break into a large account and gradually push out your competitors, the same can happen to you, too. The risk is that you develop a relationship so much that you become complacent and assume that the client will only ever buy from you. The best way to defend an account from competition is to value the account and give it the attention it deserves.

I recommend that you design formal account reviews into your service, not just as a way to find new sales opportunities, but also as a method of ensuring that the client account gets sufficient attention. We want our clients to talk to us about their problems rather than to our competitors. If we are doing our job properly, even if a competitor starts talking to a client and giving them ideas, our client will tell us all about it and get us to do the work instead.

Summary

If you want to win very large client accounts, it is better to start your relationship with a small project and then grow the business rather than trying to compete for large opportunities when you are not yet tried, tested, and trusted. You can grow a small opportunity into a significant client account through project expansion, new projects, and client expansion. Prioritising your accounts by potential will allow you to put your business development effort where you will get the maximum results for your time. Divide up your client accounts based on growth potential and set a minimum value so that you are clear as to the size of prospect you are pursuing. Give priority to 5-Star Client accounts with the highest growth potential and schedule the remainder of your client accounts around this core activity. Remember to not only focus on winning new business but also on defending your existing business against advances from your competition.

Chapter Six

Filling Your Sausage Machine

Introduction

We have now looked at the mechanics of sales; you know what an ideal client looks like and you have an insight into their buying motivation. You also understand the strategy of starting off with a small sale as a way of growing much larger client accounts, despite there being a lot of competitors offering the same services as you. Now it is time for you to start generating interest in your company's services. You need to start to fill the hopper of your sausage machine, and in this chapter I will show you how to do that without having to resort to cold calling. I will be focusing on the activities that you can do directly rather than having to rely on someone else to generate sales opportunities for you.

Walking the corridors

I remember my boss from my IT consulting days used to tell me on a regular basis that the only way to build a consulting business was through personal contacts. He would refer to it as 'Walking the corridors', the idea being that you would go to a client site and while there, you would go and see many people, say 'hello' and work on developing relationships. Conversations would be about various things and would often start with a generic question like 'How's it going?' to which you would get a myriad of replies. Often a reply would be about a problem, and occasionally it would be about something that would lead to an opportunity. It could be that the person you were speaking to was not the potential buyer of services but would let you know who to speak to, or if you asked, actually make an introduction. You can learn a lot about a company's problems by simply walking the corridors and asking 'How's it going?'

My boss was very generous and allowed me to experiment with lots of different ways to generate interest, including setting up a telemarketing team, but I had to admit that even though the other methods got some results, the biggest and fastest projects always came through walking the corridors. I now know this activity to be called networking, but there seems to be a very big misunderstanding about what networking is and how to be effective at winning business through it. I, too, made all the mistakes other people make in terms of networking when I first started my business. It was only when I realised that it was the same as 'walking the corridors' that I started getting results and this led me to write my first book, *The Accidental Salesman Networking Survival Guide*. I am not going to repeat that book here. Instead, I am going to show you how to leverage your existing relationships to generate interest in your services and start a sales conversation with your ideal clients.

What is networking?

The best way to describe 'networking' is to first look at what a network is in the context of business development. You are probably familiar with LinkedIn, and hopefully, you have a profile there. Assuming you only connect with people you actually know, then your LinkedIn connections represent your network. Your 1st degree connections are the people that you know personally. Your 2nd degree connections are the people that know your 1st degree connections. If you are connected with 200 people and each of them has 200 connections, then you potentially have access to 40,000 people. Things get very interesting when you consider 3rd degree connections. If each of your 2nd degree connections has an average of 200 connections then you potentially have access to 8,000,000 people.

LinkedIn, if used correctly, should represent your network, and networking is the activity of working your network. Networking can include a number of activities, including:

- Starting new relationships.
- Nurturing relationships.
- Leveraging relationships.

Starting new relationships

We meet new people all the time through our many different activities. In addition to work-related activities, we may belong to a sports club, go to a church, or mix with parents when we take our children to school. Networking meetings are supposed to be where people get the opportunity to meet other people, but many seem to think that networking is about going to a meeting to sell to other people. As a result they may meet people, but they do not start a proper relationship. To do that you need to **relate** to the other person and have them **relate** back. That does not happen so well if you are focused on selling, rather than just getting to know people.

I recommend you connect on LinkedIn with people you meet, and if you feel there is some rapport between you, then you should meet and get to know each other. This could be over a cup of coffee or lunch. It could even be a telephone conversation. If the other person is not interested, there is probably not much of a relationship. The other person may be one of those people who are just pitching for business and who do not see the big picture— that the real value of a network is in the connections and their ability to connect you. Top sales professionals know that personal introductions have a much better success rate over cold calling which is why they focus so much effort on referrals.

Nurturing relationships

The time consuming part of networking is nurturing your relationships. Part of the activity involves being visible and reminding people that you are still around. These days you can do a lot with online social networking, like LinkedIn, Facebook, and Twitter. However, I am a great believer that when it comes to selling services and building quality relationships, online social networking is no substitute for good old-fashioned face time, which is done in person, whether via a video call, at an event, or in a coffee house.

As with any relationship, there should be some give and take. If you only ever speak to someone when you want something, then after a while they are unlikely to want to continue to speak to you. However, if you do things for people, then they are more likely to want to return the favour. There are many types of giving, and an important one is just being someone who listens and encourages the other person.

In business networking, I encourage you to network with well-connected people. Unfortunately, LinkedIn is nothing to go by as many people send out LinkedIn connection requests without knowing each other. However, the benefit of networking with well-connected people is that you will both be interested in who it is that each other knows. Well-connected people are more likely to have important connections you can pick up, and they will be interested in gaining additional good connections, too. A good way to nurture a relationship is to make valuable connections for the other person and they will normally reciprocate if they are, themselves, a well-connected person.

Generally, the more times you meet someone and invest in the relationship, the better the relationship gets. The great thing is that well-connected people often go out to events, meaning that if you do, too, you get to meet lots of people you already know. That is a good enough reason for going to such events rather than meeting lots of new people. If you are too busy to go to other people's events, then hold your own. I often organise a curry night in the evening and invite people I know. The people who attend get to meet other well-connected people and have a good time. I get to catch up with ten people all in one go as well as enjoying a curry and great company!

Leveraging your relationships

An important part of networking is giving, but asking is important, too. People who like you will probably want to help you as long as what you ask for is easy for them to do. If you ask for a personal introduction to one of their best clients without giving a compelling reason as to why their contact might want to speak to you, then it is going to be difficult for them and they may be reluctant. It is much easier for that person to give their contact a copy of your free report or invite them along to an event you are running.

Your clients are part of your network

When you see networking as the process of generating sales opportunities rather than the process of building your network, then it is easy to overlook the fact that your clients and the various relationships you have within a client account are an important part of your network. In fact, they should be right at the heart of your network, because an introduction from a happy client to one of their contacts will go a long way to helping you win business. Clients can help you win more business in a number of ways, including:

- Call you when they have a problem they want to talk through.

- Help influence other people involved in the decision making for a larger deal.

- Give you important information about competitors in a larger deal.

- Tell you when an opportunity arises in another part of the organisation.

- Make introductions to their colleagues within the same organisation or other companies in the same group.

- When they change jobs and go to a new company, they take you with them.

- Recommend your services to contacts in other companies.

A client will be more inclined to want to help you if you help them over and above the commercial transaction. It need not cost money either; often your time and insights are just as important, especially when you are dealing with senior people. They do not often get someone they trust to act as a sounding board, and the role of trusted adviser is not just about delivering services, it's also about being there for them when they want to talk something through. In services, sales are made from problems, and so having a client talk through their problems with you will potentially turn into a sales opportunity!

Look for introducers

The next best thing to getting introductions from your clients is to get introductions from people that have trusted relationships with your ideal clients. If your ideal clients are the sort of people that never go to networking meetings, then your networking activity will be so much more effective if you seek to add quality introducers into your network. You will need to do the same kind of nurturing as previously mentioned, but getting your clients and trusted contacts to connect you to potential introducers will accelerate the nurturing process significantly.

The best introducers will have a related product or service, so that the introduction has relevance and authority. For example:

Business type	Example of a good introducer
Data quality consultant	Marketing consultant
IT support	Web designer
CRM consultant	Sales consultant
Business intelligence consultant	Part-time finance director
Data migration consultant	Data warehouse consultant

Whilst many people in your network may not be able to refer you to potential clients, they may be able to make an introduction to a good potential introducer and accelerate the relationship-building process.

An introducer may be open to making such connections for a number of reasons, including:

- To help out a client.
- In the hope that you will introduce them to some of your clients.
- For a finder's fee.
- Because they like you and want to help.
- Because they like the person who introduced you and want to help.

The strategy of 'start small and grow' helps introductions, especially if you specialise in your area of maximum credibility. It is much easier to refer a specialist than a generalist.

Turn your consultants into introducers

Many technical consulting companies have 'Finders' and 'Grinders'. The Finders are the business developers who win the work and oversee it. The Grinders are the technical consultants who do the detailed work. When you have technical consultants working on your client's site you can train them as to what kinds of problems to look out for. The best way to do this is by sharing example stories of problems you have solved for other clients. Rather than training all your consultants to sell, you just need to train them to recognise problems you can fix and maybe gather some information to help you be able to broach the subject with the client.

Competitors can be introducers, too!

There could be opportunities to win quality business leads from your competitors, especially those where you are not directly competing. For example, a website developer who specialises in large and technically complex websites might be able to get a website developer who only does simple brochure websites to make an introduction in return for a finder's fee. Such an arrangement could also work well on a reciprocal basis.

Another type of opportunity for introductions from competitors is where you are both regional specialists. For example, a company that focuses on the North of England could generate a sales opportunity in the South of England, and instead of letting it go to waste, introduce a competitor who is a regional specialist in that location, again in return for a finder's fee.

Going fishing

Finding sales opportunities is a little bit like going fishing. The hook is the prospect of your being able to solve their problem. The bait you put on the hook will depend on your prospect's primary buying motivation. People will not be interested in your services, but they will be interested in solving their problems.

In the previous chapter we looked at two examples of starting small with a specialist proposition:

Example 1: IT support for bespoke software.

Example 2: Business intelligence with financial expertise.

The business developer for the IT support company in example one should not be just looking for companies that want to change their IT support provider. They should also be looking for companies frustrated that their bespoke software is not supported. The frustration is the pain that will motivate them to want to talk to a business developer about potentially offering support cover for the bespoke software.

Likewise, the business intelligence consultants in example two should not just be looking for companies that want business intelligence consulting. They should also be looking for existing users of their specialist software who want help to develop cash flow forecasting models, or some other specific application that requires specialist financial expertise.

In both cases your introducers will have something specific they can look out for and talk to their clients about, especially if you have shared with them stories about clients you have helped to solve similar problems.

Work on your soft skills

When I first got involved with business development I was a technical consultant who had some experience of client management, but my people skills were not that well developed. I was not great at meeting new people, and I found knowing what to say in a conversation a little awkward—unless, of course, it was about my specialist subject. As well as having all sorts of hang-ups about sales, one of the biggest areas of reluctance—if I'm honest with myself—was shyness. People find it hard to believe these days, but there was a time when I did not say much! I recognised that it was a problem; my mentor helped me to know what kind of training I needed, and fortunately, I was ambitious enough to do something about it.

The bad news is that developing our soft skills training can take months and even years of personal development. However, the good news is that every time we engage with people, we have an opportunity to develop and hone our skills. There are plenty of great books that helped me develop my understanding of soft skills, including the classic *How to Win Friends and Influence People* by Dale Carnegie.

I found NLP (neuro-linguistic programming) training to be particularly effective for developing my people skills. I paid for my own training as an investment in my career, although as my skills of persuasion increased, I managed to get my company to fund my training by convincing them of the extra sales I would generate. Let's just say they were delighted with the results! I have listed some resources at the end of the book which will help you get started, and there is a lot of free stuff about soft skills and NLP on www.theaccidentalsalesman.com.

Generate interest by telling stories!

Just to recap, at the 'Generate Interest' stage of the sales process we are simply looking for clients who have one or more of our 5-Star Qualities and fit one of our Client Archetypes. We want to talk to people who have problems we can fix, and the pain caused by the problem is what creates the buying motivation. We are not looking for a sale at this stage. We are just looking for people with problems and who have an interest in fixing that problem.

We want to be seen as a trusted adviser and so the conversation should always be started with reference to their problem and not about our services. We need to get good at getting our clients and prospects to feel comfortable about talking to us about their problems. If we can be the one to help them think through their problem and show them how they can solve it, we are more likely to be the company they engage to support them through the change.

Example stories

I have been researching soft selling for almost twenty years, and storytelling is one of the most powerful soft-selling strategies and is the key to selling on an emotional level. Example stories are a type of story that is very effective at generating interest and communicating value. Essentially, you tell a story about a problem your ideal client had, how the problem impacted them, and how you helped them solve it. This type of story is an example of a client which had one of the problems your company can fix, and it is very effective at getting clients to admit they have a similar problem.

Example stories just slip into a conversation and they are like little fishing hooks. If the other person relates to the problem it stimulates a reaction; otherwise, it's just a nice story. However, if designed well it will be remembered, so that even if the client does not have that problem at present, they may remember the story if they do get the problem at a later date. Example stories are also very useful for helping introducers and consultants to know what problems to look out for.

Using one of the examples in the previous chapter, my client developed an example story about the managing director of the plastics company who was frustrated because he was looking to grow his sales, but who could not easily see what the overall sales position was—especially with regard to Eastern European sales—

due to the required software changes not being carried out. The story then ends with the new IT support company getting everything set up within two days and being able to provide support for and oversee changes to the bespoke system. Typical of example stories, I would take less than a minute to tell this particular story.

Developing your stories

We need you to build up a bank of stories to use when you are networking. You need at least one for each of the top priority Client Archetypes, and the story should be about one of your clients who had that particular buying motivation. So, for example, the IT services company in Chapter Four, who had the Annoyed as their ideal Client Archetype, would need to develop some examples of clients who came to them because they had been let down by their existing IT services supplier. They should be able to generate at least two or three good examples involving different stories but each having a similar plot:

Prospective client is let down badly by IT services supplier; the new company comes along and saves the day.

They would also develop Upgrader and Problem Solver stories.

People sometimes worry about giving out client names when telling their stories. I never include client names in my stories because they are not relevant. An example story is intended to illustrate the clients you work with and the types of problems they have rather than being a case study. As a result, names are not important, and the great thing is that you do not need permission to tell them, nor do you break any confidences. Even if you change some sensitive details of the story, it will still provide the example of the type of problems your company can solve.

If you have many consultants working for your company a facilitated storytelling session is a great way of collecting and sharing stories. Consultants learn to tell each other's stories and learn about the problems they should be looking out for when they are working on a client site.

Telling your example stories

What makes example stories so powerful is that they do not sound like a sales pitch at all because they are not about your company. They are about your clients who have had similar problems. They should not sound too polished or it will defeat the object, as you will sound like you are selling and will cause people to stop listening. They should sound no different than if you were telling someone about what you did during the weekend or on holiday.

The great thing about stories is that they are easy to remember, and you don't have to get the story right word for word as long as you get across the main points. People like to listen to stories about people like themselves and the problems they are experiencing. They should be able to relate to the person in the story, and if they have a similar problem they often will make a comment which is all you need to start a conversation about the problem. To see whether there is any interest in solving the problem you just need to ask a simple question like:

"Is that something you would like to fix?"

Where to tell your example stories

Think of your example stories as seeds that you scatter everywhere you go, some of which will fall onto fertile ground and grow into opportunities. You can spread them yourself and also give them to other people to spread on your behalf. Here are some examples of where you can tell your stories:

- When clients contact you and they ask you what you have been doing lately.

- Account review meetings.

- Catching up with previous clients.

- Seminars/webinars.

- Training/workshops.

- Networking meetings, as part of your elevator pitch.

- One-on-one meetings with business contacts.

A while back I did some work for a technical consultant who was running a series of seminars with the aim of generating sales opportunities. It was a hot topic and he had no trouble filling the room. He was getting really frustrated because, despite spending a fortune on the seminars and getting lots of excellent feedback, no one was biting. He was thinking of giving them up and doing something different. We went through his presentation and swapped a lot of the technical content with example stories, and not only did he start generating a lot of sales leads from the seminar, the feedback was that people actually preferred the new style of delivery.

Can you believe that? People actually got more information and enjoyment from listening to his example stories which were, effectively, a series of soft pitches, rather than listening to the purely technical content. And when they go back to their companies and have to explain to colleagues the value of your proposition, they will remember the stories you told and will be able to share them with their colleagues. They will be spreading your soft pitch to other people! This is why example stories are so powerful when it comes to generating sales leads from introducers, which we will cover in the next chapter.

Other ways to generate interest

Networking with clients and building a network of introducers are key activities for generating interest. For business developers, there are many different ways to generate sales opportunities, and for a full list with details you can download my special report, '21 Ideas for Increasing Sales in the Professional Services Sector', from www.theaccidentalsalesman.com. Here are a few that are easy to implement and do not involve a lot of cost:

White papers and special reports

Well-researched and professionally written white papers and reports focus on solving complex business problems. A white paper presents the problem in all its glory, and then presents the solution, as provided by you. Offering free white papers or research reports can be a powerful way to generate leads, particularly for emerging or tricky problems that people might not yet realise they need to worry about.

Authoring white papers and reports helps build your credibility as an expert and engages your audience. White papers encourage readers to make contact so that you can engage in a deep-level conversation with them about the subject. Responses to your content or requests for further information enable you to identify potential prospects simply by virtue of their interest in the topic.

If you are going to create a white paper or free report then it's worth doing properly. Poor quality content is worse than no content. First, choose your subject. The best topic to choose is one where you have lots of credibility and a number of client success stories. Ideally, this should be related to your primary sale so that you can promote it in the free report. Choose your title carefully so that it attracts interest and outlines the problem. Spend time on the title and choose words to capture people's imagination. Perhaps test a few on existing clients.

Take some time to write your draft content or outline. Meaty white papers are typically about ten pages or 5,000 words long. Find a writer/editor to help you shape your document and make your arguments clear, compelling and engaging. Find a designer to

97

make the layout clean, professional and attractive. Finally, get a professional proofreader to do a final check of the document—basic spelling errors can negate all the effort you've put in, so don't skimp on this stage. Use Elance.com to find writers, editors, designers and proofreaders, or ask your network for a recommendation.

Once you have your white paper you can contact existing clients and tell them about it. It is a good excuse to get in touch with them, and if you have chosen the title correctly you will know if they express an interest in it, that they have the problem the white paper sets out to address. You can also use LinkedIn to contact potential clients you have as connections. If you upgrade your LinkedIn account, you can also contact decision makers as potential clients and offer them a copy. Remember to let your introducers know about the white paper so that they can offer a copy to their clients.

Special events

As an alternative to producing a white paper, or indeed to complement it, you may want to run a special event around a current industry issue or problem aligned to your area of specialisation. Again, it's a great excuse to start talking to clients and prospects, and it's easier if you are inviting them as a guest. You could even do a joint event with one of your introducers so that you can split the costs. Ask all your introducers to invite their relevant contacts to your event so that it is well attended. Like the white paper, the title is critical, as interest in attending should indicate that the person faces the issue. And if they cannot attend but are interested, you can organise a meeting on a one-to-one basis.

An early evening seminar, breakfast meeting or business briefing is a great combination of face-to-face networking and free content—like personally delivering a white paper or free report.

Meeting your prospects in person allows you to start building a relationship, and the agenda allows you to steer the conversation to showcase your skills and experience. People are busy, so the mere fact that they have made the effort to attend shows a predisposition for your services.

Create an agenda that doesn't make attendees feel like they are sitting through a sales pitch; otherwise, your first seminar will be your last. Think about why people should take one, two or three hours out of a busy day to come to your seminar. Find out what's of most value to them: is it listening to an industry expert or thought leader on a specific issue, discussing best practices with a leadership panel, or networking with peers?

Ensure you have a couple of colleagues working the room and finding out more about your attendees, including why they came along and what is their specific need. This is likely to be where most of your leads will come from. You can make follow-up calls, but it is much easier to engage and speak to people when they are in the room and thinking about the subject.

To get a well-attended event you should allow two to three months of promotion, so plan dates, book rooms and send out invites well in advance. The sales opportunities will start coming in quicker than that, because you can start booking meetings with people that cannot attend.

Summary

The best way for a business developer to generate sales opportunities is by utilising trusted relationships with existing clients. As well as seeing clients as buyers of your services, you should also see them as part of your introducer network. Developing a network of introducers will make finding sales opportunities much easier. Business development involves a lot of interaction with people, and you may need to work on your soft skills to boost your confidence and effectiveness, if that is an issue.

Stories make building relationships easier and example stories are also an easy way to communicate the value of the services you offer and start a sales conversation. Example stories are about your clients and their problems and are designed to start a conversation if the other person has the problem or knows someone who does. You can use white papers and special events to make it easier for your introducers to make the introduction to their clients and contacts.

For free resources on **Consultative Selling for Professional Services**, including free mini-course, webinars, and e-books, visit **www.theaccidentalsalesman.com**

Chapter Seven

The Sales Proposal

Introduction

The discovery stage is a key element within the consultative sales process. Indeed, it is the one that most people associate with consultative selling. Yet it is merely a stepping-stone on the way to winning the sale. The purpose of discovering needs and wants is to allow us to fully understand the client's problem and to be able to provide a compelling solution. Therefore, before we look at the discovery stage in depth, we need to be clear about what information we intend to present in our proposal. This understanding will direct how we approach the 'Discover Needs and Wants' stage. In this chapter, therefore, we will be looking specifically at the sales proposal and the important information that needs to be included.

The selling starts here

We have already identified that in consultative selling, we can only begin to sell when we know specifically what we are selling and why our clients and prospects want to buy it. If we have done our job well in getting to this stage and have qualified out any sales opportunities where there is insufficient value, then there will be no need to be pushy. Instead, what we do need to do is to deliver a clear, concise, and confident proposal that conveys the value the client will be getting if they agree to go ahead, and one that illustrates that we are the obvious supplier to help them with the project. Whilst the proposal should be presented in a professional manner rather than being 'salesy', it is important to present everything in a way that we know will be compelling to the reader. In other words, we relate our solution to the client's buying motivation.

The sleeping salesman

A mistake that many people make is to assume that everything that has been said up to this point has been remembered. It is also a mistake to assume that you have spoken to everyone that will be involved in the decision-making process. Despite your best efforts, there is always the potential that someone has been overlooked. For example, there could be a finance director in the background who will be asked to assess the return on investment or approve the release of budgeted funds. If it is a large amount, it may need board approval.

Having a good, well-written proposal will ensure that you do not have to rely on other people to do the internal selling for you. Your proposal is your pitch, and if you include the recommendations of this chapter, it will make the business case for you to anyone who has not had any prior involvement in the sales discussions.

Not just a thick document

A proposal can be a weighty tome, but it does not have to be. If the proposal is for something quite simple then it could just as easily be presented in a single page document, perhaps as a letter. A proposal could, in theory, be presented verbally in the form of a presentation, although I would always include a written element to it for the reasons already stated.

It is important that we are clear that, in the context of consultative selling, the proposal is your pitch for the business and not just an explanation of what you propose to do. You have taken the time to generate interest in helping your client, or prospective client, to solve their problem. You have discovered what the problem is and why they need a solution. Now you are pitching for the business. I am not suggesting you suddenly need to turn into a pushy sales person; quite the opposite, in fact. You should have all the information you need to create a compelling business case using the information that you have gleaned up to this point. There are key elements to a sales pitch and these elements need to be included in your sales proposal.

Important elements of a proposal

When writing your proposal, you need to consider what the reader needs to understand and decide in order for them to go ahead. You also need to bear in mind that the proposal could be read by more than one person, and you need to be clear that different readers may be looking at the proposal from different perspectives. I do not want to get overly prescriptive with regard to the headings, as you may have your own internal house style for proposals. Also, when writing a formal proposal for a bid, you will probably be told what the sections of your proposal should be. Moreover, if your proposal is just a short letter, you may not even have any section headings. However it is presented, the document still needs to contain certain key elements in a particular order so that it achieves its sales function.

Introduction

The introduction is a short paragraph setting the scene as to why you are submitting a proposal. If someone is reading the document with no prior involvement, the introduction just helps to set the scene. For example, you might briefly state that the client is looking for assistance in achieving a particular goal, and that your company specialises in that area and has been asked to submit a proposal.

Current situation

This is a critical section and is often missing from many of the proposals I am asked to review. Even when it is included, it is often the weakest part of the whole proposal. The purpose of this section is to paint a picture of the goal and the status quo. Imagine the reader is an external consultant with no prior knowledge of the situation and has been asked to comment on your proposal. They need to understand the current situation, why it's a problem, and what are the consequences of things continuing to stay the way they are. In other words you are making the case for change from the status quo. Much of the content included in this section will be a summary of what you have gleaned during the discovery phase of the sales process. Whilst this section may not be long, it is effectively the backdrop against which you are presenting your solution, and in that respect it provides relevance and context against which to judge the value, suitability, and cost of the solution.

Proposed solution

In contrast to the Current Situation section, this is the part of a proposal that is normally done well. It is what you intend to deliver and may actually be in several subsections. For example, you may want to include timescales, deliverables, risks, assumptions. The danger of this section is that it becomes so detailed that it dominates the document, and as a result, the proposal loses its sales impact and some readers skip straight to the costs. If the proposed solution is quite long, detailed and/or technical, then consider what can be put into an appendix or even a separate technical document. At the very least, longer proposals should have an executive summary so that key decision makers are able to read your pitch and then dive into the detail if they need it. The executive summary will follow the key elements of a proposal, just as if you had written a proposal letter. It is, in effect, your executive pitch for the project.

Some businesses like to present options in the proposal and my view is that it is okay to do this, but if you do you should set expectations that you will be doing this. It does suggest that you have not been sufficiently thorough in your discovery, and often it is done because the person writing the proposal does not have a clear sense of the budget and so they are hedging their bets. My preference is to give a recommendation as to what you propose rather than leaving things uncertain. You can then always include some optional extras, although I would normally include them in the costs section of the document.

Costs

Once you have given the backdrop to the problem and stated what you propose to do about it, the next thing to cover is how much it will cost. If you have prepared the earlier sections well, you will have built the value of your solution in the mind of the reader so that they have something to judge the costs against. If you think it relevant and necessary you may include something about the return on investment. For example, if your proposal will result in savings you might comment on how long it will take before the savings cover the proposed costs.

Do bear in mind that there may be some internal costs that the prospect needs to incur that will impact their decision as to whether to go ahead. If it's appropriate when setting their expectations I suggest you make reference to those, too. You should also include details of any expenses and payment terms, especially if anything requires payment in advance.

I normally include the next steps in this section because it is probably the last section they will read.

Why us?

Up to now you have presented your proposal, and hopefully, made the business case for your client or prospective client to go ahead. You now need to make the case as to why they should choose you to implement the project rather than hiring a competitor—or, indeed, doing it themselves. It would be a good time to emphasise your specialist expertise in this area and any credibility that you have. You may even want to include some references. These are better than testimonials, especially if you include telephone numbers and email addresses. The reader needs to know that they can trust you and your company to deliver the solution. Remember that some of the readers of this document may not know your company as well as others. Also, if you are proposing to involve other consultants in delivering the work, they will need comfort that those consultants proposed are suitable. You may want to include consultant biographies, if appropriate.

The order

I hope by now I have made clear that the proposal is your sales pitch and that it flows in a particular order. I hope I have also shown that it will be more effective when you present your costs after you have built value, and that you only present your solution once you have clearly explained the problem and the related consequences when describing the current situation. The 'Why us?' section could go before or after the costs. I always put it after out of habit, and I think it flows better that way, but I do not think it matters too much. I would advise you to hold back on talking about your company until after you have presented the solution, as the reasons why you are the obvious company to deliver the solution only makes sense once you have stated what the solution is.

Kiss

When writing your proposal you should make your communication clear and simple so that non-technical people can understand it, too. This is why you might want to have an executive summary, or to include the detail in an appendix or a technical solution document. Another way of handling it is to ensure each section of your proposal has a summary first, followed by the detail in separate sub-sections. The bottom line is that the document needs to be understandable by more than just technicians unless you are confident that there is no one else involved in the decision-making process.

Beware of flip-flopping

One of the mistakes that gets ironed out in my MasterClass is the 'flip-flop', which is where people, during the discovery phase, drift into proposing a solution before they have completed the full 'Discover Wants and Needs' stage of the consultative sales process. They will ask a question, listen to the answer, and then start pitching based on that answer. Once they have finished their pitch, they ask another question.

It is still possible to succeed with this type of selling, especially if you write a good proposal, but you will not win as many sales as you might and you may miss some important information. The biggest reason not to do it is that to the prospect it feels like they are being sold to, and they will start to put up barriers and become a lot more guarded. I remember conducting a coaching session with a sales person from a financial investments firm who was earning £120,000, largely from commissions. He was winning one in every five of his sales opportunities and wanted to increase that to two in every five so that he could earn significantly more commissions. The mistake he was making was flip-flopping, and learning to stick to a pure consultative sales process, where he did all his selling once he had all the facts, made a massive impact on his results and earnings.

You do not have to do a proposal

A good proposal takes time and if you are going to go to the effort of creating one then my suggestion is that you write it with the expectation that you will win the project. If you get to the end of the discovery phase of the consultative sales process and you cannot see how you can add value or you do not believe that your prospective client will buy, then I suggest you tell them that you will not be submitting a proposal. Obviously, you need to do this tactfully, and it is always possible that your prospect will reveal something you have missed, which may reverse your decision.

I remember a few years ago having a meeting with the regional head partner of a well-known accounting firm who also offer business advice. The partner was telling me about his frustrations with his fellow partners and the fact that they just seem to focus on the technical aspects of accounting rather than seeking additional work from their clients. He was telling me how he wanted to have them all trained in sales and how he liked my soft selling approach, which he thought would go down well with his partners. All was looking good until I asked about his targets and he revealed that they were beating their targets and that they were actually the best performing region.

I decided to test how serious he was about the training and asked him why he thought he needed training, given his region's success. He admitted that he was unlikely to go ahead with the training and we agreed to keep in touch, although he did refer me to another region where people were having problems reaching their targets. By doing the test I discovered that creating a proposal would have been a total waste of time, and I walked away pleased that I had got to the truth and unearthed a better sales opportunity. I had also left the door open for sales training in the future, having proved my credentials as a trusted adviser rather than just trying to sell a training course.

Summary

With the consultative sales process, the real selling starts at the 'Propose Solution' stage. This is where you know exactly what the client is buying and why they will buy it. If you have qualified out sales opportunities you do not expect to win, you will stand a high chance of winning the sale. Before thinking about how to approach the discovery phase of a sales opportunity, we need to be aware of what information we need to discover in order to be able to submit a compelling proposal. A proposal should be capable of being understood by someone who has not been involved in the discovery phase and should show them that it is a good deal. A good proposal will contain the following critical elements:

- Introduction
- Current situation
- Proposed solution
- Costs
- Why us?

The proposal is your pitch, and the information should be presented in the right order. The headings are less important than the order of the content, and it is vital that this key information is included, even if you are proposing your solution in a short letter or email. The order ensures that you build value before presenting costs, so that the reader can assess the costs in the context of the value the solution will give them. With longer proposals you should have an executive summary which should contain all of these key elements, also in the right order.

For free resources on **Consultative Selling for Professional Services**, including free mini-course, webinars, and e-books, visit **www.theaccidentalsalesman.com**

Chapter Eight

Remember to GRIN

Introduction

Now that we know what makes a compelling sales proposal it is time to begin the process of discovering the specific information we need to know before we are ready to start writing our proposal. In this chapter I will show you how to handle the discovery phase and introduce you to a model that will guide you through the process of discovery.

Breaking the ice

Many trusted advisers find it easier speaking to people we already know rather than meeting new people for the first time, especially if they hold senior positions within a prospective client. It is something I have worked on and over time my confidence has grown, and it will be the same with you, too. The important thing to remember is that at that point in the relationship they are more interested in how you can help them rather than being interested in you personally. You do not need to impress them with what you know. Instead, you will impress them by being totally interested in them, their business, and their problems.

I had to learn not to get straight down to business and to spend time developing a connection with the other person. These days it happens automatically, but when I first started I had to make a conscious effort. This state of connection is called 'rapport', and it is very difficult to describe but easy to spot. If we were to look at two people talking from a distance we can tell whether they have this connection because they are probably sharing a similar body posture and making similar gestures. If we were to listen to their conversation, they are probably using similar words and speaking at a similar pace. This phenomenon is known as 'matching', and it is one of the things that naturally friendly people do without realising. It is a learnable skill and one I had to develop.

When I was learning about this and went on training courses, we were encouraged to start mimicking the body language of other people. I really struggled with this as it really annoyed me when I could see others doing it to me on purpose. I assumed that it would be the same for others. I learnt about a technique called 'Mirroring' where you match something similar and it is not so obvious to the other person. I still felt that I was being manipulative. What I went on to discover is that when we like someone else, we do this naturally and it is not noticeable because our attention is on the liking and not on the mimicking. I think it is useful to learn about matching and mirroring because it is great for feedback, but the quickest and easiest way I have discovered to get into rapport with someone else is to have a sincere interest in them and look for things in common.

When people like each other they tend to trade stories or, to be more precise, anecdotes. An easy way to break the ice at a sales meeting with someone you have not met before is ask them their story about how they started the business or how they came to be working for the company. Listen to the story and look for things you have in common. This approach works like a charm, and I always find the answers fascinating. Whilst they are telling their story you can feel the tension being lifted. You are not looking to be best buddies with the other person. You just want to get to a position where you both feel comfortable to drop your guard and have an open and frank conversation. It is hard for people to feel comfortable answering our tough and challenging questions without the existence of rapport.

.

A great time to start the rapport-building process is when we first arrive and they greet us at reception and we are making our way together to their office. They will ask questions about our journey, and I find something positive to comment on, like the building or the location, and I ask how long they have been there. I find that people love to talk about themselves and rarely get the opportunity. It is vital in consultative selling to be the one who is listening and discovering rather than the one talking. Give them the treat, take an interest in what is said, and you will find any ice quickly melts away!

Stop selling and start GRINing!

When I was learning how to sell, my mentor recommended I read *SPIN Selling* by Neil Rackham, which I found incredibly useful; I thoroughly recommend you read the book, too. The SPIN® system, of which I became a big advocate, is essentially a framework for the 'Discover Wants and Needs' stage of the sales process. SPIN is a mnemonic covering four distinct elements:

- Situation
- Problem
- Implications
- Needs

The idea is that you need to ask questions to elicit information about all four elements during the discovery stage. After using SPIN for a couple of years I got sent on a coaching course where I started to develop the skill of 'non-directive' coaching, which essentially means that you do not give your 'client' the answers but instead help them to think through their own problems and come to their own decision. It is very effective, especially where you are dealing with people who are much more knowledgeable about a subject than you are.

Anyway, I decided to see what would happen if I changed my approach from being 'consultative' to helping my clients think through their problems, using my coaching skills. Given that the discovery stage is not about giving solutions, it worked very well, and not only did my proposals get better, but also the levels of trust increased, too. To be good at 'non-directive' coaching you have to be good at asking questions that make people think for themselves. Often clients do not know what they need and our value to them is a trusted adviser and not just someone who takes down an order.

Asking good, challenging questions will get the client to think about the problems in new ways, for which they will be grateful. You always know when you have asked a good thought-provoking question because your client says to you, "That's a good question!"

The risk with models like SPIN and Solution Selling is that you just ask questions to get the answers you want to hear so that you can push your solution onto the client. I know that is not the intention of the developers of these sales approaches, but it is an easy trap to fall into unless you are suspending any judgement of what they should be buying until you have completed the Discovery stage of the sales process.

The GRIN model developed by chance not long after setting up my business. I was asked to speak to the London Coaches Group on how to sell without being pushy, and I wanted to make the point that when you do consultative selling really well it is very much like good coaching. Most coaches, at some point, learn about a coaching model called GROW, which was originally developed in the 1980s by Graham Alexander and further developed by many others. It has four main questioning areas:

- Goal – What do you want to achieve?

- Reality – Where are you now in relation to your goal?

- Options – What are your options for achieving your goal?

- Will – What action will you take?

So I took the Goal and Reality from the GROW model and the Implications and Needs from the SPIN® model to give me GRIN. It went down really well with my audience, and I started to include it in my consultative selling training courses. I found that doing role play around questions to determine the goal and reality significantly improved the skill level of attendees and fits well with the idea of doing a GAP analysis—a tool that consultants seem to understand.

Goal

Here we are looking to discover what different people want and why they want it. Rather than being a lofty future goal, it is the goal in relation to this sales opportunity. Another way of putting it is to ask what your client's objectives are. They may have a problem currently, but what do they want instead? What would things be like if the problem were to disappear? Sometimes the problem is that they want to achieve a goal and they are not progressing fast enough or something is preventing them from achieving it. If this is the case then it is important we know what the goal is, why the goal is important to them, and how things will be different once they have achieved their goal.

I find that most people who come on my Consultative Selling MasterClass are good at asking clients and prospects what they want, but do not stop to find out why they want it. As we have seen previously, understanding the primary buying motivation is vital information if we want our solution to hit the spot.

Reality

With Reality we are seeking to understand the status quo and where people are in relation to their goal. We want to find out what they have previously done to achieve their goal and the results they got. Why does the problem persist and how is it impacting the business? What would happen if nothing were to change and the problem continues into the future? Will things remain the same? Will things get better if they did nothing? Or, get worse?

When we understand the Reality of the client's situation we establish the value gap when we compare it with the client's Goal. What is equally important, and where the coaching comes in, is that the client needs to have the value gap in their mind, too. It is not enough that we see the problem. They need to see and feel the problem; otherwise, why would they want to do anything about it?

There will be a cost of maintaining the status quo, and the higher the cost, the more likely they will be motivated to do something about it. Your careful questioning should remind them of the pain, but you want them to tell you how painful it is—or let you know as quickly as possible that there is no pain. If there is no pain and no desire to fix the problem, it is unlikely that there will be any motivation to pay for a solution.

Implications

With Implications, we are seeking to determine the value gap. We want to know how people will benefit from achieving their goal and what would happen if they were to continue with the status quo. The value of the solution is the difference between the two outcomes. With a simple sale we could discover the goal, the reality, and the implications in a single conversation. For other opportunities it could take a series of conversations with several people in order for us to gain that information.

Up to now we have mentioned buying motivation, and we probably have not been too specific about price. We need to find the reasons why they will still want to buy once we present them with the costs.

Once you have the Goal and the Reality, you should start to get a sense of the value gap between what they want and what they will have if things continue without change. The thing that will tell us what it is worth for the client to do something about the gap will depend on the implications of them reaching their goal compared to the implications of them maintaining the status quo. When we start to explore implications we begin to determine the kind of information that will give us a sense of the return on investment they are likely to achieve.

The return will come from comparing the changes in revenue and costs of the two courses of action. From the perspective of return on investment, the avoidance of a future cost counts as part of the project income as much as a future increase in income. The costs of any solution will need to consider the internal costs of change even though they may not be included in your proposal. These costs should include both financial and emotional costs. This is because it will determine whether or not there will be the internal will to proceed with a solution. You do not want to go to the trouble of writing a proposal if there is unlikely to be the political will to go ahead.

Needs

Whilst the needs tend to flow from the goal, the reality, and the implications, I also find it useful to ask whether people have an idea of what the ideal solution might look like. I learnt about this in the book *The New Conceptual Selling* by Robert B Miller & Stephen E Heiman, both of the highly esteemed Miller Heiman organisation, where they suggest that prospects sometimes have a sense of what the solution looks like and it is worth asking just to check. This ensures that when you present your solution it either matches or you know you need to set expectations.

An example of this happened early in my business when I was invited to meet the chief executive of an organisation that sells law books to lawyers, who wanted some training in consultative selling for his sales team. From the discussions it was looking to me like two days of sales training—a basic course, followed by a more advanced course the following month. When I asked him how he saw the training going, he mentioned that he thought it would be half a day a month for six months, and he told me why doing half days was important as he wanted to do other product training on the same day. Finding out what he had in mind meant that I could ensure my solution was aligned with his needs.

20 questions

On my Consultative Selling MasterClass we look at questioning skills at a more advanced level, and I play a game I call 20 questions to show people what is happening when they ask closed questions during the discovery phase. I tell the group that I am thinking of somewhere in the world and they need to guess where it is. Now, bear in mind that by the time we do this they will have already watched a video and taken a quiz about advanced questioning skills, and in particular, open questions. Yet it normally takes at least 10 questions before they cotton on that they are not getting anywhere by asking closed questions like:

- Is it in the Northern Hemisphere or Southern Hemisphere?
- Is it in Europe?
- Is it well known?

Instead they could ask more useful questions like:

- Where specifically is it?
- What does it look like?
- What would I do there?

To a certain extent I set people up to ask closed questions by asking them to guess. What is happening is that they imagine somewhere in the world and then ask a question to see if they are correct. This is what happens a lot in selling. We guess what prospects' problems are and then ask closed questions to see if we are right. Instead of trying to *guess* what they are thinking, we should be finding out what they are **actually** thinking. By asking well-chosen, clear and open questions, we will get the information we need, and in addition, perhaps more important information that they would never have otherwise volunteered. Also, when they give an answer we may want to ask a more detailed follow on question about something they have said.

Closed questions are useful for confirming that you have correctly understood what people have said or if you want them to make a decision. Learning about open and closed questions will not help improve your questioning skill. It's only by being clear as to the information you need and then purposefully choosing the best question to get that information that you will improve. On our MasterClasses we do lots of exercises where attendees get feedback, and we find that gradually, by the end of the day, they are consistently asking good questions. After that it's down to them to continue to practise in the days and weeks after the training until they are so used to it that it starts to be an automatic behaviour.

GRIN is a framework and not a process

It is quite easy to think of GRIN as a process. It seems logical that Goal questions would be followed by Reality questions, leading you to discuss the implications of each. In practice, what tends to happen is that the lines get blurred because when you ask a good, open question, you often get information that covers more than one area. For example, someone may tell you about what they are looking for and why they want it, or there may be an ideal opportunity to ask why something is important when they mention it rather than coming back to it later. The objective is to discover the value gap, and the GRIN framework helps you to think about the types of things that you need to ask, rather than all the questions being neatly in any set order. After a sales meeting, I get a piece of paper and divide it into four boxes, one for each element of GRIN, and I start to write out all the information I have obtained on each of the four areas. That helps me to know if I have enough information or whether I still need more.

Planning your discovery questions

I recommend that you take some time before a sales meeting to prepare and to think about what you want to know. From a brief qualification call you should have some information as to why the prospect has expressed an interest in talking. This should tell you what Client Archetype they are, and from there you should have some idea about what information you want to know and what questions you need to ask in order to get things going.

For example, going back to our IT services example in Chapter Four, if we were going to see an Upgrader then, in addition to some of the technical things we might ask them, we might also like to know things like:

- What services are included in their current IT support contract? (Reality)

- What types of additional services are they looking for? (Goal)

- Why are they important? (Implications)

- How will they benefit from having those services? (Implications)

- What quality of service are they seeking? (Goal)

- How does it differ from what they currently get? (Reality)

- Why is that extra quality important? (Implications)

- What impact is the current situation having? (Implications)

- How will that change with the improved service levels? (Implications)

- What do they like about their current supplier? (Reality)

- Why is that important? (Reality)

- What would they most like to change? (Needs)

- What kind of service levels do they want? (Needs)

You can see that in this example there are some blurry lines between whether a question is a Goal type question or a Needs type question. The Needs will often arise from the meeting. This is not important in this example as we are trying to build a sense of a value gap rather than being a slave to the model. In other sales opportunities most of the questions will be focused on the current situation and understanding the problem and why it is a problem. The Goal and Needs will arise as a result of asking the more detailed questions about the problem and seeking to establish the value gap.

A discovery meeting can be conducted over the phone

I used to think that discovery meetings needed to be conducted in person. Having face-to-face contact is much better, but if you already have a trusted relationship then there is no reason why the questions cannot be asked via telephone or Skype. In the 'Discover Wants and Needs' phase you may need to speak to several people, and with modern communications it is much easier for people to connect remotely. If you have never done any work for a client then you should aim for a face-to-face meeting, perhaps after an initial telephone conversation. If you only speak on the telephone whereas your competitors meet the prospect in person then you will be at a disadvantage.

Who is the decision maker?

In larger companies and with larger projects there could be more than one person involved in making the ultimate decision. You need to understand how the decision will be made and by whom it may be influenced. Ideally, you should be speaking to those people who will have the biggest influence on the final decision. There is only ever one person who makes the ultimate decision on whether a sales proposal gets the go ahead. I like to call this person the 'ultimate decision maker'. This is the person who can say 'Yes' when everyone else says 'No' and 'No' when everyone else says 'Yes'. Interestingly enough, who the ultimate decision maker is will depend on the size of the project, whether it is planned expenditure, and the level of authority required for that type of expenditure. It may not be as easy as going by job title.

You should aim to speak to the ultimate decision maker, although if they are very senior, they will most likely delegate the meeting to someone else. This does not mean they have delegated the ultimate decision, but only that they have delegated the task of doing the groundwork to get to the decision. The person you are now dealing with is probably going to influence the outcome, but will not make the ultimate decision. You need to keep the ultimate decision maker included in communications, so that you keep that line of communication open should you need it.

Other people who can influence the decision could be:

- Project managers
- Internal and external consultants
- People who the project will impact
- Finance
- Professional buyers
- Legal people

It is important to map out who will have a major influence on the decision and include them in your sales activities.

Example

I used to sell IT consulting services for planning and forecasting systems, and we would supply skilled consultants to create a forecasting system for the client's business. The finance director would normally be the person who would ultimately pay for the consulting work. We would also have to speak to the accountants who would be using the system. Most of them would be addicted to MS Excel spreadsheets, and our solution would mean that they would have to abandon their spreadsheet approach and use another system. I had to get these accountants to buy-in by finding their buying motivation in the same way as if I were selling to the ultimate decision maker. They would not stop the project from going ahead, but they would be important for ensuring that the project ended up being a success. They also could provide useful information about the kind of detail that the finance director either didn't know or maybe didn't think it was important to mention.

Another thing to be alert for is that one of the key influencers could prefer one of your competitors. Maybe they have worked with them previously, or they could even be friends or be related. You need to know if someone with influence is working against you rather than just being neutral.

Getting inside information

One thing that could really help you to understand how the land lies within a larger account with added complexity is to find a champion who really wants you to win and is able to help you understand the more subtle aspects of what is happening behind the scenes and what the potential buying motivation is. As you win and grow accounts, finding a champion becomes easier as you get to know more people. The best person for this is normally someone who is not a key influencer in the decision-making process, but who knows the people who are and who wants you to get the work.

Summary

The aim of the discovery phase of the consultative sales process is to 'Discover the Wants and Needs' of your prospects to enable you to write a compelling proposal. At this stage you are discovering the difference between the situation your prospect is seeking and their current position. The difference between the two is effectively the value they will achieve by getting the solution they want. The four elements of the GRIN model are:

- Goal

- Reality

- Implications

- Needs

The GRIN model provides a framework for eliciting the information required to write a compelling proposal. You are looking to find the impact of achieving their desired goal compared to the impact of continuing with the status quo. To get the best results from the GRIN model you need to see yourself more as a coach helping the prospect clarify their thinking around their buying decision rather than trying to sell to them. Using open questions will help you be more effective and get to the information you are seeking much more quickly.

For free resources on **Consultative Selling for Professional Services**, including free mini-course, webinars, and e-books, visit **www.theaccidentalsalesman.com**

Chapter Nine

Winning the Sale

Introduction

So far in this book we have looked at buying motivation and how we engage in a sales conversation with our clients and prospective clients. We have helped them to think through their problem and to discuss their needs and wants, and we have delivered a compelling proposal. The sale, however, is not complete until we get a decision. Closing the sale is something that many people struggle with, and in this chapter I will help to demystify the close and help you deal with some of the issues that arise when trying to win a sale.

Always be closing!

There is a lot of misunderstanding around the technical aspects of sales that I would like to clear up, at least as far as they concern the selling of professional services. Many of the books I have read on sales (and believe me, I have read over 300 and counting) give the impression that the objective in sales is to close the sale. They also give the impression that closing the sale is synonymous with winning the sale. Of course we want to win the sale; otherwise, what would be the point. However, in consultative selling there are several closes rather than just one.

When I talk about closing the sale, I am talking about ending one stage of the process so that we can either progress to the next stage or stop spending any more time on that specific sale, whilst still nurturing our 5-Star Client relationships. Once we are sure that we are talking to the right people and that there is a good fit to what we are offering, then we should do everything we can to win the work. However, to damage the trusted relationship in the process by suddenly getting pushy is like cutting off your nose to spite your face. Here is a little story that makes the point:

> A man and his wife owned a very special goose. Every day this goose laid a golden egg, which provided a very comfortable income. Some days it laid more than one egg. On occasions it laid no eggs at all. The couple, however, had lived very comfortably from the golden eggs.
>
> One day the man was looking at how to improve his finances and was wondering where he could get more money. "Just think," said the man to his wife, "if we could get to all the golden eggs that are inside the goose, we could fulfil all our dreams right away!"
>
> "You're right," said his wife, "just think of how much all those golden eggs would be worth. Why wait?"
>
> So, the couple killed the goose and cut her open, only to find that she had no golden eggs inside of her at all. That was the end of their daily golden eggs.

Your objective in selling professional services is to start small and grow. You want to keep your existing business whilst seeking new sales opportunities. Being pushy will quickly damage your trusted relationship and put at risk the whole account. It is not always easy when there is pressure to win more sales, but in my experience, trying to push a sale through the consultative sales process never ends well. What you can do is look for ways to motivate a client to move more quickly through the process, but it needs to be powered by their motivation rather than tricks and techniques. The secret is to get really good at filling your sausage machine with quality opportunities and being quick to qualify out any sales opportunities which are not going anywhere. In other words, get good at the earlier stages of the sales process and the latter stages will become much easier to do.

Each new piece of business won should be celebrated, and whilst we need to have targets, at the same time we need to respect, nurture, and service our clients. Equally, we must not be so worried about our trusted relationships that we never undertake any business development activity except when our client asks for help. This is referred to as 'order taking', and whilst some opportunities may eventually come to you without trying, it is a risky strategy to take and being reactive in this way often leads to the 'feast and famine' syndrome we discussed in Chapter Two. If we take a professional and proactive approach to sales and we follow the consultative sales process we will have happy, loyal clients. We will also be very successful overall, even if one particular client is not spending as much money with us as we might like.

When one door closes another opens

To recap the consultative sales process for professional services, there are seven stages:

1. Generate Interest
2. Qualify Interest
3. Discover Wants and Needs
4. Propose Solution
5. Negotiate Solution
6. Ask for the Business
7. Deliver the Promise

I would like you to imagine that you are staying in a very large hotel and you are walking along a corridor. It is a circular hotel and if you were to keep on walking then you would end up back where you started. As you are walking along this corridor you notice that there are fire doors every so often, and that as you pass through a door it closes behind you. You keep progressing until you reach the next door.

Now, relating this to the consultative sales process, you should be seeing each door as a decision whether to proceed any further. It is a decision that your clients and prospects will make and also a decision that you make too.

At the **Generate Interest** stage you decide whether to take action and your client decides whether to agree to a sales conversation. When you agree, then you have both left the **Generate Interest** stage and walked through the door into the **Qualify Interest** stage, and the door behind you has closed.

When you are happy there is a good fit and your client agrees to allocate some time to talking in more detail about their business problem, then you have both passed through the door into the **Discover Wants and Needs** stage, and the **Qualify Interest** door closes behind you.

When your client requests a proposal and you feel you have enough information to submit a good one and so you agree to it, then it is time for you both to walk through the door into the **Propose Solution** stage. You remember the choice is yours as to whether to write a proposal and the choice is also the clients as to whether they want to progress any further with discussions. The **Discover Wants and Needs** door is now closed and you are proceeding to the next door, which is when your client has received your proposed solution.

The **Propose Solution** door is now firmly closed and you are in the **Negotiate Solution** stage with your client. When you and your client have agreed on a basis under which you are both happy to proceed and you have a verbal agreement, then it is time for you both to leave the **Negotiate Solution** stage and walk through the next door to the **Ask for the Business** stage.

The **Negotiate Solution** door swings closed and the **Ask for the Business** stage, which is normally very short, finishes when you and the client get the paperwork done and you both walk through the next door into the **Deliver the promise** phase, closing the **Ask for the Business** door behind you.

When the agreed work has been delivered to your client's satisfaction, and they have met their payment commitments, it is time to walk through the **Deliver the promise** door to find yourself at the **Generate Interest** stage once more.

It is very important that with every sales opportunity you know what stage you are at in the consultative sales process. You should know what activities you need to undertake and what criteria will tell you that you have left one stage and entered the next. You should also know that there is no point in trying to take a sales opportunity forward if there is not going to be sales revenue at the end of it. At any stage the sale could come to an end because either you or your client decides not to proceed through the next door.

Objections demystified

In sales terminology, objections are issues that clients and prospects have with a proposal that holds them back from wanting to proceed. I prefer to think of them as 'reservations'. There are a number of things that can cause a client to not want to proceed, including:

- You have not qualified the opportunity correctly.

- You have missed a vital piece of information.

- You have not presented the information well enough.

- The client has misunderstood your communication.

- The proposed solution does not match what the client is looking for.

- It's not a good deal for the client.

- The client has a better alternative.

- The client does not believe you can deliver.

- The client does not like you.

As you can see, there are many reasons for the client to not want to proceed. They are sometimes voiced, but often you will not get any response at all. Getting the earlier stages of the consultative sales process right will reduce the number of objections you get, and I am going to focus on how you can both minimise them further still and also handle any that do arise so that you end up getting a deal you are happy with.

Price objections

Given that you have been qualifying the opportunity from a very early stage and have checked for a ballpark budget, there are a number of reasons why people will still object to price at this stage.

They cannot see the value

The problem here is normally that the client is unable to clearly see what they are getting for their money. One proposal I reviewed recently for a company selling IT services was full of technical jargon, and there was no mention of the current situation. It transpired that the existing supplier had caused significant problems by not responding quickly enough to a support call. Something that was quite simple to fix ended up having expensive consequences which caused them to want to change their supplier. The IT services company's rates were only a little higher than the existing supplier and it should have been easy to make the case that the little bit extra is worth the peace of mind. Putting in some guarantees around their service-level agreements would probably have been enough to charge even higher prices and still win the business.

Sometimes I see the right information in the proposal, but it is buried somewhere in detail. You should always make the value clear and put it early in the document—remember, the value comes from contrasting the impact of the solution with the impact of maintaining the status quo. The price should always come after you have built the value and not before, because if the price is unexpected at that point, you are going to have an uphill battle to get the buyer's attention. In short, tell them why they need what you are proposing, what you are going to give them, and then tell them what it will cost. Ideally, the return on investment should be clear without needing precise numbers—what I call a 'no-brainer' return on investment.

They are not comparing like with like

Another common mistake I see when reviewing proposals is that the reader is unable to make an adequate comparison with alternative proposals because some of the relevant detail is omitted. In my experience, this is often caused by the writer of the proposal assuming that the client already knows that information. That may be true, but it is easy to forget if they are considering several potential suppliers and it is better to be safe than sorry. I always write a sales proposal as if there will be someone I have not met reviewing my sales proposal and judging it against alternatives as well as considering the option of doing nothing.

They cannot afford it

In my early days of selling I lost a deal because the client said they could not afford it. They did not have enough budget. I was very surprised to find out later that a competitor won the project and the client had spent even more with them; the sales person had sold at the senior level and they had found the money by raiding other underused budgets. The bottom line is that if people want something badly enough, they will find the money. We need to be speaking to all the people involved in the decision, and we need to get comfortable with talking about money and budget. We should definitely know before writing the proposal that there is money available, even though we may not know the precise amount required until we have written the sales proposal.

They want to negotiate

Some companies will have professional buyers whose job it is to negotiate the lowest price possible. If you get that far, and it is not part of a formal tender, it is a good sign that the client wants your solution and they probably want you—they are just haggling over the price. If you are not aware of this and familiar with the techniques that professional negotiators are trained in, it can be quite a daunting experience and one I remember only too well!

I have since been professionally trained in negotiation and on the tactics buyers use, and it's something I recommend if you are having to get involved with buyers. If your first sale is small, as recommended, then they probably will not bother with the buyers.

One thing to be clear about is that with professional negotiators it is not personal. They do not really care about you or your solution. Their job is to get the best deal for their employer. Consequently, they have a vested interest in getting your fees as low as possible, and you can assume they will be prepared to use every trick at their disposal to achieve that. Rarely are they the final decision makers, and if you are confident both of your pricing and their next best alternatives then it will be a case of holding firm and weathering the storm.

Sometimes it is not only the purchasing managers that have been trained in negotiating skills. Senior managers may have been trained in negotiating skills and will want to negotiate. In some companies it is expected that everyone will.

The most common negotiating tactic you will face is what is known as 'flying a kite' and tactics include:

- Saying that you are more expensive that your competitors.

- Telling you they never pay more than £X.

- Telling you they want to proceed but you need to do something about the price.

- Telling you that the budget has been cut.

The technique is used for just one purpose—to get a reaction. They know that most people involved in sales are naïve when it comes to negotiating and this is the easiest way to get the price they want. They just fly their kite and the unsuspecting business developer simply caves in and drops their price. If this is your first sale with a client, your biggest defence is your specialty and expertise. You know they are interested or they would not be negotiating. My best advice is to be prepared to change the solution but avoid changing your day rates. If they want a lower rate, then offer them a less skilled person to do the job. Another option is for an internal person to do some of the work so that the number of hours required is reduced. If you reduce your rate for this project you will set a precedent for subsequent projects.

If they are unable to agree to your day rates then you may decide to walk away from the project. You want clients that are focused on the overall cost rather than being fixated by day rates. Going into a negotiation knowing you are prepared to walk away from the deal puts you in a much stronger negotiating position. You need to know what you are prepared to change, what else you can include if needed, and what you expect in return. Never give away anything without getting something in return if you want to be seen as a trusted adviser rather than just a supplier.

They have a better alternative

It could be the case that your client has preferred alternatives which include doing it themselves or doing nothing. You should have picked this up during the discovery phase, and if it was a likely outcome (i.e. you would have done that if you were in their position), then you probably should have declined to submit a proposal. If they raise a price objection it probably means that they are still interested but are looking for you to match the alternative. Remember not to give away anything without getting something of equal value in return. It is unlikely that the alternative matches your proposal 100% so there could be room to reshape your proposal so that the profitability is maintained.

Handling price issues

If you get involved with setting the costs in your proposal then you should really be aware of the market for your professional services. This includes the costs of the contract market and the likelihood that the prospect could easily find someone else to do as good a job as you will do. A key dynamic in the buying decision is risk and people will pay more for certainty. My best advice is to be clear about your pricing policy and then be confident you are able to defend it. If you decide to price above market rate, then stick to it and know how to justify it. Make it an asset. In Europe we currently have advertisements for a beer called 'Stella Artois' and the slogan is 'Reassuringly Expensive'. Either be above market rates or be competitive. I would advise strongly against ever trading on the basis of having below market rates. There is the risk that people will assume that you are less competent than your competition. Once you decide on your pricing policy, do not negotiate your rate, but always be prepared to negotiate the project.

There are a number of things you can do to alter the cost of the project, including:

- Use less experienced staff (may increase risk).

- Use client resources for some of the tasks.

- Reduce the scope of the project.

- Prioritise deliverables into 'Must do', 'Should do', and 'Could do'.

- Phase the project so that some of the work gets put into a future phase.

As you can see, it can get very tricky to negotiate this type of thing at this late stage of the sales process, and this can all be avoided if you take time to know the client, know what the client's alternatives are, and anticipate their reactions when you write your sales proposal.

The long 'No!'

One thing that often happens when we do not take care to handle the earlier stages properly is that when we get to the 'Negotiate' stage the prospect goes from being very engaged and interested to becoming very hard to reach. When this happens, there is a high probability that they have decided not to proceed or have given the work to someone else. Alternatively, they could be very busy and consider that there is no hurry to proceed now they have your proposal. This is the one stage in the whole consultative sales process where things can seemingly get stuck. At this point we need to know where we stand in relation to the sales opportunity and get some dialogue. The typical sales approach is to start pushing, making repeated calls, and sounding more and more desperate with each one. I recommend the opposite; send an email or leave a voicemail message assuming you have not won the project. For example:

Hi Sarah,

I have not heard from you in a while about the XYZ project and I assume you have decided not to go ahead with our proposal. Thanks for the opportunity and I look forward to speaking soon.

Best wishes,

Richard

One of two things is most likely to happen:

1. Sarah will respond, admitting that we have not won the work, or to say that she has decided not to proceed, in which case we can discuss it and maybe talk about alternative solutions or approaches they can consider in the shorter or longer term.

2. Sarah will respond saying that she has been very busy but that they are still interested, and perhaps suggesting a time to next speak.

Either way, you will have returned to dialogue and you will be clearer as to where you stand and what the next steps are. Please note that the wording in the email above is an example rather than suggested wording!

Negotiating the solution

The 'Negotiate' stage does not necessarily mean that you will be embroiled in a formal negotiation until the early hours while you hammer out a deal. If you have handled the earlier stages of the sales process well then your client may just accept your proposal verbally. The negotiation could be as simple as agreeing to a start date. Some people like to put options in their proposals and then negotiate which of the options that the client wishes to go for. This is quite common if the business developer has not discovered what kind of budget they have. As a trusted adviser I want to give my recommendations to a client, but I do sometimes add some optional extras, if appropriate. Like, for example, if I am doing an in-house training workshop, I might suggest that they buy a copy of my book for each attendee. If it were essential, then it would be in the core recommendation, but otherwise it would be an optional extra.

One of the key skills in negotiation is to be able to see things from the other person's perspective, anticipate what they want, and find a way of giving them what they want whilst getting what you want, too. In my view, the time to anticipate is when you are writing your proposal rather than having to waste time on negotiation or risk having your proposal rejected. Standard sales training has objection handling as a key feature and yet, if you conduct the earlier stages of the sales process well, those objections should not come up and there will be no need to negotiate.

I prefer to refer to objections as 'reservations' and a regular reservation business developers face is price. The price is either too high or it is too low. The latter would be a credibility issue and the client is unlikely to tell you about this. If the price is too high then something has gone wrong in qualifying the opportunity and with setting and understanding expectations of pricing. The proposal should match expectations and this is a skill that comes from experience and mentoring. When it comes to negotiating on price, my golden rule is to negotiate the solution but not the day rate. Once you have proposed your day rate then you should stick with it. Anything else is a negotiation about the solution.

Getting agreement

A sale is not won until the paperwork has been done. There needs to be a formality that can be as simple as getting an email confirmation or a purchase order through to getting the client to formally sign a proposal. Many a sale has been lost by business developers relying on a verbal agreement. The verbal agreement is a good start, and in my experience you need to ask for the business rather than waiting for the client to say they would like to go ahead. We just need to get in the habit of asking for the go-ahead and then asking for the paperwork.

What you need to do is to find a way you are comfortable with routinely asking for the business that fits with what you are selling. For example:

- "Would you like to go ahead?"

- "Shall I sort out the paperwork?"

- "Would you like me to book you in?"

In traditional sales literature, this is referred to as a 'trial close', and by asking the question you will know where you stand so that you know how to proceed. It is when you ask the question that any objections will surface and can be dealt with.

If you sense that the client or prospect is a little unsure then you could do a 'soft' close. You mention that you want to be sure you are able to meet their deadlines if they were to decide to go ahead and ask if they would like you to pencil in some dates. Assure them that they can cancel or say you will let them know if you need those dates for someone else. What you are aiming for is either a 'Yes', a 'No', or a reservation that you can deal with.

Summary

Rather than thinking of closing the sale as a specific action, you should all the time be thinking about what needs to be done to close the current stage of the sales process so that you can either progress to the next stage or decide not to continue. The consultative sales process is something that is done with your clients and prospective clients rather than something you do to them. There are various activities to be completed at each stage before the sales opportunity is ready to pass to the next stage. It is important that you are always aware of what stage in the sales process you are at for each of your sales opportunities.

After you have submitted your sales proposal there is a stage at which you may need to negotiate the shape of the solution. Hopefully, you will have anticipated any potential cost issues when writing your sales proposal, but these and other changes will be made during the Negotiate Solution stage. When you have finalised the proposal you need to complete the sale by asking for the business and to get the paperwork done. If you have followed the earlier stages of the consultative sales process and you are seen as a trusted advisor then this should be a formality.

For free resources on **Consultative Selling for Professional Services**, including free mini-course, webinars, and e-books, visit **www.theaccidentalsalesman.com**

Chapter Ten

The Road to Mastery

Introduction

Up to now you have learnt a lot about consultative selling and you can see that it's possible to carry out selling activities alongside your billable consulting work. Unfortunately, just like in sports, you cannot develop skill just by reading a book. You develop your selling skills through experience. What's more, experience in sales is no reflection of mastery. What if you had twenty years' experience of doing the same thing ineffectively? In this chapter I will show you how to develop your consultative selling skills so that you not only quickly become effective, but you begin to master them and start to enjoy the consultative sales process.

Practice makes perfect

If you want to be effective at sales, you need to move beyond just doing the same thing over and over again. The closest analogy for developing your selling skill is learning to drive a car. I can remember when I learnt to drive. It all felt a bit strange and awkward at first, but after a while I got used to it, until everything came naturally, and I didn't even have to think too much about it to get where I wanted to go. Imagine if I just continued to drive in exactly the same way as I did on my very first lesson—never learning from my mistakes, adapting, and getting input from others.

An important part of learning how to drive is to have a driving instructor. The instructor will draw your attention to what you did well and also what you need to do differently. When you are engaged and talking to clients and potential clients in a sales situation, you will no doubt do it to the best of your ability, but without external feedback you will be unlikely to improve significantly. It is hard to review yourself unless you have a video recording of your sales meeting or an audio recording of your telephone conversations. Even then it is not perfect at the earlier stages of development because you may not yet know what *good* looks like. However, if you take someone with you to your sales meetings who is there to provide feedback, you will be able to adjust your style and behaviour next time and start to develop and fine tune your skill.

Even if you are very experienced at sales, having someone to observe and give feedback is going to make a big difference to accelerating your skill improvement. A key element of my Consultative Selling MasterClasses is realistic role-play from which you get feedback and suggestions as to how you can do things even better. It is only by acting on the feedback that you develop and fine-tune your skill.

Early in the development of my consultative selling skills, I would follow my mentor everywhere and just sit in on his sales meetings and watch and learn. I would ask him why he said or did certain things and why he did not do or say other things that I normally did. Sometimes I would drive him to meetings just so I could ask him questions. He then kindly came with me on some of my sales meetings and just sat and observed without getting involved. Before the meeting we would agree the objectives and afterwards we would have a debrief, where he would tell me what I did well and what I could do differently next time. This is exactly the scenario I recreate in my MasterClasses and sales training workshops. Getting a mentor will help you accelerate your learning process dramatically. If you have a colleague who is successful at consultative sales who will mentor you, that is a great place to start. I know one very successful IT consulting company that makes mentoring a key part of the job function for principal consultants, although funnily enough, they do not mentor each other on consultative selling skills. Getting someone from within your company to mentor you is ideal provided they are familiar with what good consultative selling looks like. If that is not possible then you may want to consider getting your company to pay for some external mentoring. Again, it should be with someone who knows what good consultative selling looks like.

Embrace sales

My best advice, especially if you are currently very nervous or fearful of sales, is to embrace it. Recognise that business development is an important part of career development in the world of professional services and developing the skill will make you more valuable, and give you additional career options too. If you want to be successful in running a business, being able to sell is essential. Not only do you need to be able to grow the business, but you also need to persuade talented people to come and work for you, suppliers to give you special terms, and banks and investors to give you funding.

One of the great, added benefits of developing your selling skills is that they come in handy in lots of other areas. For example, getting colleagues to buy in to your ideas will become much easier. I managed to get my employer to pay for a lot of my NLP training when I had developed my selling skills enough to realise how easy it was to get people to agree to my plans. Pay raises were easy too! Another hidden benefit is making more friends and improving the quality of personal relationships. Just imagine getting your children to clean their rooms and do their homework, whilst also passing on the skills that will help them get on in life.

Learners are earners

Even if you are in the business of delivering your own services, I encourage you to take a professional approach to sales. It took me seven years to develop my management accounting skills to get to a senior level. In three years of continual self-directed learning I managed to dwarf what I used to earn as an accountant in sales, and I still managed to do plenty of paid consulting—which is my real passion. I realised that to do more of what I love doing I would need to get better at winning and developing my own clients or be forever reliant on others who did not have my own best interests at heart.

When I learnt to be an accountant I did not just read one book and assume I knew it all. I spent a fortune of my own money on accountancy manuals, evening classes and crammer courses. I had to take exams twice a year, and I either passed or failed. With sales there is no test other than cash in the bank! The great thing is that you do not need to invest in manuals and classes unless you want to. The kind of books I needed for accountancy were not available in the library. Fortunately, most of the books you need are either available free from the library or at low cost from companies like Amazon. You can get a lot of free information online. My own website provides free recorded interviews with many sales and marketing experts, and there is lots of free stuff on YouTube.

If you are short of time for learning, then audio files are great, especially if you do a lot of travelling. You can get audio versions of many of the classic sales books, and you can listen to them whilst driving or travelling on the train as an alternative to listening to music. Most mobile phones these days have the ability to play audio files, and Amazon owns the website www.audible.com, which is a great source for audible books.

If you are lucky like I was, you can even get a talented business developer to mentor you for free. I have had many mentors over the years, all of whom have mentored me for free, and I have over the same period always mentored two people for free to return the favour. If each person who gets mentored goes on to pass the knowledge to two more people, then increasing numbers of people will get the benefit of the privilege I had. I did have to pluck up the courage to ask. These days I enjoy mentoring young people who are looking to embark on a career in sales. I reckon if I can teach them how to sell with respect and integrity and they go on to mentor others to do the same, then slowly but surely, the sharp sales practices will become a thing of the past.

I have to say that after seventeen years of being in sales I am still learning new things all the time that are improving my results and the results of my clients. It's the classic case of the more you know, the more you realise you don't know. I have given away more sales books to charity than many struggling sales people have read in their lives. They may have a natural flair for sales, but they have done nothing with that talent. People like us can easily win against such sales people when we develop our skills.

Little and often

The great thing about sales is that you don't need to read loads of books to get started. The learning will help you become more effective at getting results. The strategies outlined in this book will make a significant difference, but if you struggle with the softer skills like empathy, communication, and relationships, like I did in my early days, then you will need to work on them. Empathy helps you to gain insights into how your prospects are thinking and feeling. It also is important in developing relationships and is the ability to build rapport and get people to trust you. If you cannot communicate in sales, then you are in trouble.

I was really weak in all those areas, but because my mentors told me I had to continually work on those skills, I did. I did it every day. I would read for fifteen minutes a day, every day, and spend the rest of the day putting what I learnt into practice. Fifteen minutes a day, every day, soon adds up! Over the course of a year it is ninety-one hours, which is the equivalent of eleven days of education a year. Once I started getting results, I shifted up to thirty minutes a day, plus the time I was spending with clients.

My first mentor told me that if I sought to increase my effectiveness by just 1% a week because of compound interest, over the course of a year it will be more than a 50% increase. Indeed, over three years a 1% improvement in performance results is an improvement of around 350%—no matter what level you are starting from. To me that was very exciting, and it took the pressure off. As long as I got into the learning habit and continually looked for what I could do better, I would consistently improve, and it continues to be the case to this very day. Indeed, I spend more money on my own personal development than some companies spend on their whole team!

Just like when you learn business, accounting or any subject, there are ancillary subjects that have a big impact on the effectiveness of sales techniques. Over the last seventeen years I have studied lots of different things to do with relationships, communication, and personal effectiveness. Communication alone can become a lifetime study if you want, and it's the same with relationships and influence. I focus my attention all the time on what is going to give me the best return on my efforts. As I write, I am focused on my public speaking and making my talks more entertaining. Public speaking is a great way of lead generation and the more entertaining I can make my speaking, the more speaking engagements I will get.

See yourself as a learner business developer

Confidence is a major asset in sales. When you feel confident in what you are doing your clients will have more confidence in you and your services. Conversely, when you are lacking in confidence with sales, your clients can misinterpret it as you lacking in confidence that you can deliver. One idea that has been successful with my mentoring clients is to get them to see themselves as learner business developers. They imagine they have a learner driver 'L' plate strapped to their chest and back, and that gives them permission to make mistakes.

The reality is that the learning becomes very enjoyable and it quickly goes beyond sales techniques into understanding people, behaviour, communication, and all sorts of things that help us to be more effective in life, not just in sales. Unlike with learning to drive, once you get the learning bug you never remove the 'L' plates. You just keep on learning and developing, and as a result, you become more masterful at sales, more influential, and more persuasive.

The accelerator and the brake

In Chapter Two I told you about the sales sausage machine and we looked at the hopper, which is where you put your potential sales opportunities, and then the barrel, which is the process you apply to the sales opportunities. The third aspect we did not cover is the handle, which represents activity. Most technical consultants have no desire to be sales people and yet to progress their career they need to get involved in business development. As a result, you are probably not as enthusiastic about sales, which could impact your activity. If you want to feel in control of sales and feel confident when you are in sales situations then I recommend that you focus on increasing your activity.

There are two dynamics of sales activity which I refer to as the *accelerator* and the *brake*. Motivation is like the accelerator in a car and drives our sales activity. Just like when driving a car our speed of progress can fluctuate. The more we put our foot down on the accelerator, the faster we go. Fear and lack of confidence, on the other hand, work like the brake on a car and slow things down. We could have one foot right down on the accelerator, but if the other foot is firmly on the brake the car is unlikely to be going anywhere fast.

Focus on the prize

It is easy to look at the sales activity as hard work and think that you would rather be spending your time doing consulting projects. There are two ways of looking at sales activity. You can look at it in terms of the work that needs to be done, or of how that work is going to benefit you personally. If your aspirations are for career advancement, then focus on how your life will be different once you achieve your career aspirations. This is about focusing on the prize. When I got to principal consultant level and started to enjoy the extra earnings, I did not want to go back to just being a technical consultant. I also wanted to be able to provide even more for my family in the future.

The other way to look at your sales activity is to focus on the price of sales activity. In the early days it will undoubtedly feel uncomfortable, and there will be disappointment at losing deals and making mistakes. If all you do is focus on the price of your sales activity, it will sap your energy and your enthusiasm. Believe me—I've been there. It can be easy to get drawn into considering the price from time to time. Funnily enough, it's normal when things are not working out how you want them to. You never feel that way once you have won a big deal; the price is long forgotten.

The way my mentor explained it to me is that there are two mountains. The first mountain is your goals and what you want to achieve—the prize. Behind that mountain is another mountain—the price. When the prize mountain is small, all you can see is the price mountain. What you need to do to stay motivated is to make the prize mountain so big that it totally blocks your view of the price mountain.

I find that many people, even top sales people, are not actually motivated by money. They are motivated by what they want for themselves, their family, and the people that are important to them. These, of course, require money and yet are things that drive the motivation. Having a clear plan to achieve the personal goals increases the motivation even further, and that motivation will drive your sales activity.

What we need to get massive amounts of sales activity is to have massively motivational goals, whilst taking our foot off the brake.

Massive Goals

My friend, David Hyner, is a speaker and author on massive goals, which he learnt from interviewing top performers from business to sport to show business. Consistently, across the board they all believed in having massive goals. I recommend you check out David's work in the resources section.

One problem I had for many years is that I knew I should have goals, but I secretly struggled to know what I wanted. However, I could wax lyrical about what I did not want. So one day I started to list out what I didn't want. I got a long list and then, one by one, I thought about what I wanted instead. Before long I had a long list of goals, and then I was able to prioritise them based on which of them were most motivational and also which were most important to me.

I tell you this because many people I work with also struggle to set goals, which is why they do not have any, despite being told they should have some. If this is you, then do what I did and list out everything you don't want in your life, then think about what you want instead—and make your goals big. David Hyner told me that not one of the people he interviewed had realistic or achievable goals. They all set really hairy goals that were both exciting and scary. Then they did something really important. They broke the goals down into smaller chunks and started doing something towards achieving them straight away.

Get yourself some WOW! goals

We all know the importance of personal goals, but they are not always motivating. I first discovered the power of WOW! goals when running a goal-setting workshop for a client. The group was doing the exercises, and yet the room was lacking in the kind of buzz and excitement you would expect when people have highly motivational goals.

I asked one person what would be the one thing that would be so motivational right now that it would make her go 'WOW!' She replied that she would like to take her family to Las Vegas and to take a particular roller coaster ride there. Just by talking about it her face became full of emotion and excitement. I could tell it was motivational for her, and I am pleased to say she did get her roller coaster ride!

At the time, though, she was a little confused about the type of motivational goals we were talking about. She could have afforded to go on the trip anyway, without reaching any targets. I managed to convince her to only allow herself to book the trip once she had reached her sales target, even if she could afford it. As well as having massive goals I also recommend you set some WOW! goals, too. By setting emotionally charged short term goals and hitching them to the achievement of your important sales targets, you will get the motivational drive to power the sales activity needed to achieve both your WOW! goals and your massive goals.

So what would make you go WOW! just to be thinking about it? A nice new watch? Taking someone special to tea at the Ritz?

Making a large donation to a cause close to your heart? It is most likely that the goal will not be business related but something to do with what is most important in your life, such as family and friends. As long as the goal makes you go WOW! there are no rules. If the idea of organising a staff coach party to Margate does it for you, then go for it!

It's normally better that your WOW! goals are smaller and achievable rather than something grandiose. If taking your kids out for a McDonald's meal is a luxury, but would give you immense pleasure, then that is all it takes. As long as you can commit to not allowing yourself the goal until you have reached your target, then it does not matter how small it is.

The ideal plan is that you will have a whole string of WOW! goals stretching out across the year in sequence and tied into achieving specific sales targets. Targets can be more than just actual sales invoiced. If finding new clients is a particular issue for you, then why not set a WOW! goal for when you win your first sale from a new client?

If you want to increase your number of clients from ten to twenty, why not have a WOW! goal to mark that achievement? Once you achieve your target, make sure you follow through with the reward. They will not work if deep down you know that you will not reward yourself. If money is an issue, make sure the reward is financed by the sales results and make each successive target a bigger WOW! goal.

Get a game plan

Someone told me once that a goal without a plan to get you there is delusion. There are a lot of people that have watched the movie *The Secret* and are sold on the idea that if we just visualise our goals they will manifest themselves. The bit they left out is that there is work involved and if we take action towards our goals, then we can make extraordinary progress.

Set your goals in concrete and your plans in sand

When we pursue our goals, things do not always go according to plan. Rather than adjust our goals we should simply adjust our plans. Once you have your personal goals, you should be dovetailing them with sales goals so that in reaching your sales goals you will be moving closer to your personal goals.

Summary

Mastering consultative selling takes time and experience. Skill takes time and lots of activity to develop, and you need to be continually working on honing your consultative selling skills. Your skills development may well extend beyond technical selling skills into softer skills, such as relationships, communication, and influence.

Embrace sales and be clear about how all areas of your life will benefit from developing your selling skills. Commit to continual learning and consider getting a mentor to help give you feedback so that you can fine tune your skill level. Work on your goals and stay focused on them so that the work involved in developing your skill will seem small in comparison. Work out a game plan for how you will reach your goals, and remember to tie it in to your sales activity so that you get the accelerator effect and your foot comes off the brake.

For free resources on **Consultative Selling for Professional Services**, including free mini-course, webinars, and e-books, visit **www.theaccidentalsalesman.com**

About the Author

Richard White is a sales improvement consultant who specialises in enabling technology companies to sell more professional services. He is an inspirational speaker for professionals and business owners who hate the idea of selling. By sharing his personal story and his insights, Richard changes the way people think about sales and inspires them to start to take a more structured and proactive approach to finding and winning profitable new business.

Richard holds an MBA from Cranfield School of Management, where he specialised in the marketing of services. He worked as a business intelligence consultant for over ten years, starting off at Oracle and going on to become a principal consultant for an Oracle partner, building a successful consulting practice with clients like Unilever, First Choice, and British Airways.

Richard is a Master NLP Coach and Master NLP Practitioner and is skilled in helping technically minded people feel more comfortable about sales. He is known as The Accidental Salesman®️ and is the founder of TheAccidentalSalesman.com.

Richard is a recent convert to trekking having fulfilled a lifetime ambition of visiting Machu Pichu in Peru. He is also a regular visitor to the cinema and enjoys dinner parties with friends.

You can contact Richard at rwhite@theaccidentalsalesman.com

Resources

There are hundreds of free articles, audios, videos, and e-books on networking and other sales and marketing related topics for accidental sales people at:
http://www.theaccidentalsalesman.com.

Like other thought leaders, I stand on the shoulders of giants. Over the last twenty years I have attended countless trainings and read hundreds of books which have all impacted my philosophy in some way. Below I list some of the books that have made a significant impact on my thinking in relation to the topics covered in this book.

SALES

SPIN Selling by Neil Rackham, McGraw-Hill, Random House, 1988.

Solution Selling by Michael T. Bosworth, McGraw-Hill, 1995.

The New Conceptual Selling by Robert B Miller and Stephen E. Heiman, Kogan Page, 2011.

The New Strategic Selling by Robert B Miller and Stephen E. Heiman, Kogan Page, 2011.

Non-manipulative Selling by Dr Tony Alessandra, Fireside, 1992.

Zero-Resistance Selling by Maxwell Malz, Dan Kennedy et al, Prentice Hall, 1998.

Soft Sell by Tim Connor, Sourcebooks, 1994.

Relationship Selling by Jim Cathcart, Perigee, 1990.

The Trusted Advisor by David Maister, Charles Green and Robert Galford, Simon & Schuster, 2002.

The Psychology of Selling by Brian Tracy (Audio CD), Nightingale Conant, 1995.

Successful Selling with NLP by Joseph O'Connor and Robin Prior, Thorsons, 2000.

Sales on a Beermat by Mike Southon and Chris West, Random House, 2005.

LEAD GENERATION

The Accidental Salesman Networking Survival Guide by Richard White, www.bookshaker.com, 2011.

The Gorrillas Want Bananas by Debbie Jenkins and Joe Gregory, Lean Marketing Press, 2008.

The World's Best Know Marketing Secret by Ivan Misner PhD, Virginia Devine, Bard Press, 1999.

Masters of Networking by Ivan R. Misner PhD and Don Morgan MA, Bard Press, 2000.

Seven Second Marketing by Ivan R. Misner PhD, Bard Press, 1996.

Business by Referral by Ivan R. Misner PhD & Robert Davis, Bard Press, 1998.

Networking for Life by Thomas Power, Ecademy Press, 2003.

And Death Came Third by Andy Lopata and Peter Roper, www.Bookshaker.com, 2006.

RELATIONSHIPS

How to Win Friends and Influence People by Dale Carnegie, Simon & Schuster, 1981.

How to Have Confidence and Power in Dealing With People by Les Giblin, Prentice Hall, 1956.

Making Friends by Andrew Matthews, Media Masters, 1990.

COMMUNICATION

Made to Stick by Dan and Chip Heath, Arrow Books, 2008.

NLP at Work by Sue Knight, Nicholas Brealey Publishing, 1992.

Never be Boring Again by Doug Stevenson, Cornelia Press, 2003.

Unleashing the Ideas Virus by Seth Godin, Simon & Schuster, 2002.

All Marketers are Liars by Seth Godin, Penguin Books, 2007.

The Tipping Point by Malcolm Gladwell, Abacus, 2001.

Sleight of Mouth by Robert Dilts, Meta Publications, 1999.

OTHER

The Acorn Principle by Jim Cathcart, St Martin's Press, 1998.

The 7 Habits of Highly Effective People by Stephen R. Covey, Simon & Schuster, 1992.

Awaken the Giant Within by Anthony Robbins, Pocket Books, 1992.

Unlimited Power by Anthony Robbins, Simon & Schuster, 1989.

Predictably Irrational by Dan Ariely, HarperCollins, 2008.

Grow your Service Firm by Robert Craven, Crimson Publishing, 2011.

The Massive Goal Principle by David Hyner (audio) available at www.goalsettingaudio.com.

Printed in Great Britain
by Amazon.co.uk, Ltd.,
Marston Gate.